volunteer IOWA
SEEING IMPACT PROJECT

AMERICORPS IOWA

TABLE OF CONTENTS

Preface
5

Introduction
11

Iowa AmeriCorps Reading Corps, United Ways of Iowa
17

AmeriCorps Partnering to Protect Children, Iowa State University-
Child Welfare Research and Training Project
35

Youth Achievement AmeriCorps Program,
United Way of East Central Iowa
67

AmeriCorps 4-H Outreach Program, Iowa State University-
Extension and Outreach, 4-H Youth Development
83

Green Iowa AmeriCorps, University of Northern Iowa-
Center for Energy and Environmental Education
97

A Commissioner's Response
111

PREFACE

Kristin Honz
Senior Program Officer
Iowa Commission on Volunteer Service

This monograph focuses on AmeriCorps State programs administered by the Iowa Commission on Volunteer Service (commission or ICVS), one of fifty-two state service commissions that administer 75% of AmeriCorps State & National funding. The mission of ICVS is to improve lives, strengthen communities, and foster civic engagement through service and volunteering. This mission, in part, is carried out by the work of ICVS' AmeriCorps State programs. In Iowa, the commission is a learning organization focused on strengthening the ability within our programs, including AmeriCorps, to work better. What "work better" means to us is that the AmeriCorps programs: a) provide high quality experiences to the AmeriCorps members, b) engage community volunteers in their work and c) address community needs or challenges through service and volunteerism.

AmeriCorps is a National Service program where individuals, known as AmeriCorps members, commit to serving significant amounts of time to addressing community needs. AmeriCorps members serve within the structure of an AmeriCorps program, which is operated by a nonprofit, government or faith-based organization or a collaboration of these organizations working together. These organizations represent public-private partnerships wherein federal funding comes from the Corporation for National and Community Service through a competitive grant process and local funding comes from a variety of sources.

The goals of the AmeriCorps program are: (1). Getting Things Done - by providing service to address community problems; (2). Strengthening Communities- by uniting individuals and institutions in a common effort; (3). Encouraging Responsibility- throughout members' service experience and throughout their lives; and (4). Expanding Opportunity- by enhancing members' educational opportunities, job experience, and life skills. The purpose of AmeriCorps State is to engage AmeriCorps members in direct service and capacity-building activities to address unmet community needs. Local programs design service activities for a team of members serving full- or part-time over the course of one year or during the summer. Sample activities include tutoring and mentoring youth, assisting low-income persons in accessing resources, building homes, and restoring parks. AmeriCorps members also mobilize community volunteers and strengthen the capacity of the organizations they serve. The organizations that receive grants are responsible for recruiting, selecting, and supervising AmeriCorps members to serve in their programs.

As organizations that receive federal funding, our AmeriCorps programs are under increasing pressure to demonstrate the value of their work through evidence-based interventions and by evaluation. Whereas in the past, AmeriCorps programs were able to use performance measure data to demonstrate the impact of their work, this no longer meets the requirements of the Corporation for National and Community Service. In order to respond to these increasing requirements, ICVS is seeking to improve capacity for using evidence-informed and evidence-based interventions and to demonstrate impact via evaluation. While the federal government is placing heightened emphasis on proving program models, the commission's primary goal for evaluation is to help programs obtain information that will enable them to continuously improve their program.

ICVS has utilized a multi-focused approach in an effort to strengthen the capacity of our organization to respond to increasing federal requirements. For example, staff has participated in numerous training webinars and sessions designed to increase our working knowledge of the evaluation process and the federal evaluation requirements. ICVS has called on the expertise of researchers in providing technical assistance, conducting reviews and providing training. And we have engaged an evaluation expert to guide our programs through an evaluative process. The result of this evaluative effort is contained in this monograph, the final reports from the Iowa Seeing Impact Project.

Seeing Impact Project is an experiential learning method designed for programs to learn while they do. This model was selected by the commission for several reasons: 1) cost, 2) capacity, and 3) ongoing support.

First and foremost is cost. In Iowa, an AmeriCorps program receives an average of $243,000 in federal funds, while the median federal funding level is only $185,658. This level of funding is generally not sufficient to conduct a high-level evaluation. For the Seeing Impact Project, ICVS was able to utilize state formula funding to support the project costs and this allowed programs to participate without the financial burden. The experiential learning design allowed the programs to gain the knowledge to conduct their own evaluations and build processes to continue to conduct evaluations and improve their program over time.

Secondly, SIP supported capacity building and sustainability for programs by utilizing a team approach to conducting the evaluation. In Iowa, the majority of our program directors are the only person paid with federal funds on the grant and many program directors do not have experience with evaluation. With most nonprofits facing 20% turnover annually (Nonprofit HR, 2014 Nonprofit Employment Practices Survey) it is important to have more than just one person with the knowledge and capability of leading and conducting evaluation efforts. Furthermore, the team structure also allowed for more interviews in a shorter period of time and offers the ability to conduct the evaluation and generate a report in less than one year. This allows programs to benefit from the information and put new initiatives and processes into place for the following grant year.

In addition, the experiential learning model allowed the programs to receive ongoing support and technical assistance from our contractor throughout the process. Because the model allowed for a mix of in-person and web-based training, the teams received a great deal of education and information about evaluation generally and about this model specifically. In addition, throughout the process, the teams received one-on-one assistance and guidance on their theories of change, interview protocols, quantitative surveys, themes/findings and reports. This technical assistance allowed for errors to be corrected relatively quickly and kept the teams on track with their efforts. The education, technical assistance and support helped bolster the confidence of the evaluation teams and really helped them understand the value of the findings and recommendations. Since Seeing Impact Project involved a cohort of teams, the teams developed a rapport with each other and were able to learn and grow from interaction and sharing among the teams. The combination of peer and professional support was a powerful way for programs to increase their capacity for evaluation.

As a commission, Seeing Impact Project has enabled us to learn more about Iowa's programs and expand understanding of the work they do. Commissioners were able to observe the SIP presentations and read their reports and commissioners indicated that this was a valuable experience in increasing their understanding of the AmeriCorps programs and service of the members. Seeing and hearing the passion and excitement program associates have about the work that they do and how evaluation has informed efforts to improve programs has renewed the commitment of our staff to support and assist the programs as they work to grow members and address community needs. As participants in the training sessions, commission staff expanded our knowledge of evaluation and built internal capacity to support programs in their evaluation efforts. Commission staff has seen summary results of Seeing Impact Project evaluation efforts from Oregon and Washington and have noticed some similarities in findings. Analysis of similarities across programs and states is an area for further exploration.

We commend Iowa's programs for this important work and express our gratitude to Steve Patty, Ph.D, our consultant on the project, who made evaluation interesting, engaging and understandable. We also express our appreciation to Nancy Franz, Ph.D., our Iowa expert whose support and knowledge have been invaluable to Iowa's evaluation efforts. This important evaluation effort was financially supported by the Corporation for National and Community Service.

INTRODUCTION TO THE PROJECT

Steve Patty, Ph.D.
Dialogues In Action, LLC

The aim of the Seeing Impact Project is to develop in the leaders of Iowa AmeriCorps programs the ability to design and implement self-studies of their impact.[1] As such, it is a capacity-building project. It includes a number of modules which are delivered both in person to the cohort and through webinar to the individual organizations over the course of six months, as well as coaching and feedback for the critical elements of design along the way.

The Seeing Impact Project takes teams of leaders from AmeriCorps programs through a process of discovery. The idea is to develop the ability to see and communicate the effects of the programs on the people they are designed to serve. There are three primary movements of work to the project: (1) Intended impact, (2) Inquiry, and (3) Implication. Each of these is guided by instruction and coaching.

The project begins with a focus on the work of identifying and clarifying the intended impact of each of the participating programs. Once the ideas

---

[1] This project is not designed to provide an experimental or quasi-experimental version of impact evaluation. Instead, it is an effort to upgrade the existing capability of each organization and give them to tools to gather data on the attributed impact both qualitatively and quantitatively from the subjects they serve.

have been developed, and indicators have been identified, the teams then design a questionnaire to collect data about quantitative measures and a qualitative interview protocol to collect qualitative data. These data are analyzed. Themes are developed and then translated into findings. From the findings, the teams develop program responses and communiques.

PROJECT DESIGN

The fundamental elements of the Seeing Impact Project follow the traditional arc of evaluation design:

Part 1 - Intended Impact

This project begins with the identification and clarification of what effects are intended through the work of each of the projects. Each team develops an articulation of intended impact to include the components necessary for evaluation design.

- A. Main Ideas of Impact

  Each team identifies a few ideas of impact that frame the intention of direct impact for the program. In some cases, these ideas are mapped in relation to the secondary and tertiary impacts of the program to gain clarity about the fundamental notions of desired effect as a direct consequence of the program or service rendered.

- B. "What We Mean"

  From these primary ideas, the teams then develop a brief explication of the meaning of their ideas of impact. This takes the ideas that are occasionally technical and translates them into a communication that is accessible to all.

- C. Quantitative Indicators (E3)

  Quantitative indicators are then identified for each of the ideas. The aim is to generate five or six of the most critical indicators for each idea, paying attention to the data power, proxy power, and communication power of each of the key ideas. As well, the intent in this step is to identify a range of cognitive, affective , and behavioral indicators that can be measured through a questionnaire.

- D. Qualitative Indicators (E4)

Qualitative indicators are also identified in this stage. These are the articulation of the structural and qualitative elements of growth and development that signal progress on the key ideas of impact. The qualitative indicators become the basis for the protocol construction for the in-depth interviews in the inquiry phase.

Part 2 - Inquiry

In the inquiry stage of the project, each team designs and implements a strategy for data gathering. These take two forms: a questionnaire to collect quantitative data and an in-depth interview to gather qualitative data.

A. Quantitative Data and Analysis

For each of the E3 indicators, an item is designed for a questionnaire. Since these projects are not intended to provide experimental or quasi-experimental inquiry, the attribution of effect is built into the questionnaire items. The questionnaire is deployed, in most cases, to the entire population of recipients to the program services. The data are analyzed using measures of central tendency. The teams then design displays of the data for rendering in their SIP report.

B. Qualitative Data and Analysis

The development of a qualitative design encompasses a number of steps, including the following:

1. Protocol Design. Each team designs an in-depth interview protocol that uses the Heart Triangle method of question design. These produces a protocol of about nine sequences of questions (18 questions in total) to be used as a guide for seeking data about the awareness and reflection of subjects' structural shifts and developments of growth and progress.

2. Sample. Each team identifies a sample of subjects using a purposeful stratified technique to identify a selection of subjects representative of the population being served.

3. Data Collection. Interviews a convened, most lasting between 45 minutes and 1 hour in length. Data are collected via notes

during the interview, and then augmented immediately following the interview to provide a substantive rendering of the interview.

4. Data Analysis. Team members apply a four-step model of analysis to each of the interviews. This process provides them with a casual version of coding and interpretation, illuminating the primary themes from each interview.

5. Thematics. Through a guided and facilitative process, the entire data corpus is then examined. Themes are mapped through meta-analysis of the emerging insights.

Part 3 - Implication

The intent of the project is not to leave teams simply with a report about their program's effects, but rather to use the insights from the evaluation to guide the further development of the program. This takes two forms:

A. Program Adjustments

The team then takes each of the findings from the evaluation and considers possible program adjustments informed by the discoveries of the evaluation. This keeps the evaluation relevant for program application and improvement.

B. Program Experiments

In addition, the teams work to identify potential design experiments that they might run as an implication of the insights gained through the evaluation.

In this stage, the teams also begin to develop a report of the evaluation findings as well as other possible communiques of their discoveries to staff, stakeholders, funders, and other members of the community.

PROJECT RATIONALE

The development of evaluation capacity is takes time and iteration. It requires both instruction and practice – training in some of the leading techniques of research accompanied by ongoing applications and practice. This project recognizes the power of partnership, the enrichment of cross-pollination of ideas among like-minded organizations, the durable

Introduction

impact of a learning community, and the potential inspiration for a sector when exemplars are developed and elevated.

The Seeing Impact Project exhibits these unique features:

- Incremental instruction. Time is needed to gain competency and durability of learning.
- Practice. Techniques of evaluation need to be practiced to ensure capability and competence.
- Cohort-based. Leaders can learn from other organizations, even those with different missions.
- Team oriented. A small team of 3-5 helps the learning permeate organizational culture.
- Elevating exemplars. The broader community of nonprofits benefits from seeing illustrations.
- Cost-effective. This model provides maximum value for the investment.
- Proven curriculum. The curriculum strikes a balance between rigor and accessibility.

EXPLANATION OF THE REPORTS

The reports of the organizations are included in the following discussion. These will include highlights from the three movements of the Seeing Impact Project. For each participating organization, there will be an explication of the primary findings from the evaluation accompanied by the programmatic responses of strategy and design.

IOWA AMERICORPS READING CORPS, UNITED WAYS OF IOWA

Melissa Simmermaker

INTRODUCTION

From October – August 2015, the United Ways of Iowa project impact team worked to develop, for the first time, procedures for conducting a qualitative evaluation of AmeriCorps member experiences in the Iowa Reading Corps AmeriCorps Program. Prior to participation in the Seeing Impact Project, United Ways of Iowa conducted two member questionnaires, provided at the midway point and in the final month of members' terms of service, to evaluate program impact and member experience. Participation in the Seeing Impact Project allowed the team to develop a more thorough and thoughtful way for staff to understand the program's impact on AmeriCorps members. This report presents our findings and offers recommendations based on a series of interviews that were designed to get at the deep and profound impact of AmeriCorps service that we are seeking to influence within our members.

PROGRAM OVERVIEW

The Iowa Reading Corps AmeriCorps Program, a strategic initiative of United Ways of Iowa, works collaboratively with schools and United Ways to maximize opportunities for communities to access evidence-based reading initiatives to support the tremendous work of educators in our state. Iowa Reading Corps is replicating the successful, evidence-based model, first launched in Minnesota in 2003. The model is now being replicated in eleven states and uses the latest research on reading intervention strategies and guidance from literacy experts to provide what struggling readers need - individualized, data-driven instruction, one-on-one attention, well-trained AmeriCorps members serving as Elementary Literacy Tutors, instruction delivered with fidelity and the frequency and duration necessary for student achievement.

In partnership with local United Ways and school districts located across the state, the Iowa Reading Corps AmeriCorps Program launched in the fall of 2013. In its inaugural year, the program placed 10 full-time AmeriCorps members in eight school districts to provide one-on-one literacy tutoring to K-3 students who are below grade level in reading. For the 2014-15 program year, Iowa Reading Corps doubled its reach to place 22 full-time AmeriCorps members and one half-time member in 19 school districts. As momentum for the program continues to grow, Iowa Reading Corps is on track to place more than 60 AmeriCorps members in nearly 40 school districts for the 2015-16 program year. In addition to providing full-time tutoring services throughout the school year, our AmeriCorps members also partner with local United Ways and school districts to provide literacy-based services to students in the summer months to help combat summer learning loss.

METHODOLOGY

For the purpose of the Seeing Impact Project, we conducted phone interviews with 12 current Iowa Reading Corps AmeriCorps members and one alumnus. While our initial goal was to conduct interviews with each of the 22, current Iowa Reading Corps AmeriCorps members and all 10 alumni, scheduling conflicts and time constraints prevented the team from reaching this goal. Of the 13 members who were interviewed, 12 members were female and one member was male. Each interview lasted approximately 30 minutes and was facilitated by Melissa Simmermaker, Iowa Reading Corps AmeriCorps Program Director. Members serving in schools located in both rural and urban communities were interviewed. The interview questions focused on the following topics:

Development of Leadership Skills

- Positive perception of ability to make an impact in one's community
- Development and application of new skills
- Strengthened sense of self and commitment to leadership through ongoing community/volunteer service

Development of an Enduring Commitment to Community Service

- Commitment to a "lifetime of service" following a member's term of service
- Strengthened investment in bettering one's community and meeting the needs of others
- Strengthened sense of community engagement and belongingness

In addition, a quantitative, end-of-year survey was also completed by the 22 Iowa Reading Corps AmeriCorps within their final two months of service. The report was completed anonymously by members through an electronic survey system as an end-of-year program requirement. The results of the quantitative survey are included throughout this report to supplement the qualitative findings.

FINDINGS

Based upon a thorough analysis of each interview transcript, we have identified six findings that provide deeper insight into the service experiences of our Iowa Reading Corps AmeriCorps members. While some of the findings reaffirmed our initial hypothesis regarding member experience, others were quite surprising and illuminated areas of our program that need to be strengthened. To accompany each finding, staff brainstormed recommendations for continual improvement and program development.

Finding #1 – Going Beyond the ABCs

Description

Iowa Reading Corps is a K-3 tutoring program that focuses upon providing targeted literacy practice, through the use of prescribed literacy interventions, to students who are below grade level in reading. In most cases, students who receive Reading Corps tutoring are not eligible to receive supplemental services, such as special education, but are not responding at 100% to core classroom instruction. To bridge this gap, Iowa Reading Corps AmeriCorps members provide daily, one-on-one, 20-minute tutoring sessions to a caseload of 15-20 students.

Weekly progress monitoring data collected by members drives the decision-making process of making changes to tutoring sessions or exiting students from Reading Corps.

While our program focuses solely upon students' literacy outputs and outcomes and trains AmeriCorps members to complete tutoring interventions with fidelity, one somewhat unexpected theme that emerged from the qualitative research centered upon the emphasis that members noted in the personal growth (including an increase in confidence) and development of their Reading Corps students. While members understood that the program formally measures student achievement in terms of literacy outputs and outcomes, many members highlighted that their greatest achievements centered upon witnessing an increase in student confidence and the development of meaningful relationships:

> "Being one-on-one with the kids was huge. Their confidence just shoots up and you see that they're really starting to get it and make progress toward meeting their goals. I got the chance to watch one of my former Reading Corps students read aloud in front of his entire classroom – seeing his self-confidence grow was so incredible."(Male, first-year member)

> "My greatest accomplishment has been making some connections with kids who just don't connect with most other adults. It's so exciting to see that change and see kids open up and be themselves around me." (Female, first-year member)

> "Seeing the kids who first came to me not that exited, leave the program really excited about reading was a big accomplishment. Those moments when things started to click for them

and their confidence really started growing. I also think a lot of those accomplishments came from just being there for my students. They know if they need someone to talk to, they have a safe space with me." (Female, first-year member)

Furthermore, 100% of Iowa Reading Corps AmeriCorps members agreed on the end-of-year quantitative survey that the Iowa Reading Corps program had a positive impact on students.

Significance

While Iowa Reading Corps provides extensive, literacy-based training to AmeriCorps members and is, at its core, an evidenced-based tutoring program, it is apparent that our members develop relationships with their students that transcend the traditional, tutor-student dynamic. In many cases, members seemed to describe informal mentoring relationships that developed with their students. While the focus for these members still centered upon providing tutoring sessions with fidelity – it is significant that many members also noted more "extraneous" factors that are not directly addressed by our program, such as increased student confidence and positive relationship development, as significant achievements.

Our Response

Iowa Reading Corps will continue to emphasize, through training and staff support, the role of AmeriCorps members as trained literacy tutors. However, we will also explore the following options to further support and train members to address student achievements and impact beyond the program's literacy focus by:

- Providing training for AmeriCorps members in positive youth development.
- Conducting a needs assessment to measure changes in student confidence throughout their enrollment in Reading Corps.
- Structuring "share outs" for AmeriCorps members to reflect on their impacts with one another.
- Providing continued training and reporting regarding "mentorship" outcomes.

Finding #2: Moving Beyond Surface Level Growth

Description

Full-time Iowa Reading Corps AmeriCorps complete a minimum of 1700 service hours throughout their 11-month term of service. Throughout the school year, members serve at least 40 hours per week at their assigned Reading Corps school and then transition to serving with community or school-based academic enrichment programs throughout the summer months. Members also complete an intensive, three-day literacy training and a suite of monthly trainings on topics related to communication, civic engagement, volunteer management and disaster response and preparedness throughout their term of service. With opportunities for training and professional development built into the AmeriCorps term of service, we anticipated that members would report at least a base level of personal growth as a result of this experience. However, throughout the qualitative research portion of this project, we were surprised to learn that many members experienced a deep and resounding sense of internal growth and fulfillment throughout their term of service.

Because members serve at elementary schools, they are held to the same standards of professional behavior as teachers and support staff. They must also learn to navigate the educational system to professionally collaborate and communicate with teachers and internal coaches. By serving within this particular service environment, many members noted that the experience not only helped them become more self-confident, but pushed them outside of their comfort zones to find their own voices. For other members, the experience provided reaffirmation of their career goals or helped them uncover a new path to personal and professional fulfillment. Specifically, members noted:

> "I've become so much more confident in my own abilities this year. I've come out of my shell a lot, but there's still more there – I see people who I admire who say exactly what they are thinking, but sometimes I just hold back a little. I sort of got my feet wet with exploring leadership opportunities this year. This

year will remind me to continue pushing myself because I do have a voice and what I have to say is important, too." (Female, first-year member)

"Ever since I was little, I wanted to be a teacher. This experience has motivated me to keep on pushing toward that goal. I want to keep making an impact on students and ensure that they have access to a good education. I'm so much more proud of myself after this year – it's inspired me and pushed me out of my comfort zone." (Female, first-year member)

"This whole experience has pushed me out of my comfort zone as a leader and professional. For me, believing in yourself is so tied to leadership and it makes me push myself to be better. To be able to share your skills with kids and other teachers is so energizing and I thinking that I want to stay in the educational field when I'm done with my term. These kids have touched my heart." (Female, first-year member)

Furthermore, 18 of our 22 AmeriCorps members strongly agreed that serving with the Iowa Reading Corps AmeriCorps Program had a positive impact on their lives. The remaining 4 members agreed with the statement.

Significance

This finding is significant because it demonstrates that the program can have an even greater impact on our AmeriCorps members than we had originally anticipated. While we anticipated that members would grow both professionally and personally throughout their term of service, we did not expect members to express a sense of fulfillment and more sustained personal growth as a result of their term of service. As an AmeriCorps program, we have an opportunity to intentionally strengthen the components of our program that focus on the personal and professional development of our members. While we focus heavily upon ensuring that members are prepared to provide tutoring interventions with fidelity, we can also focus upon ensuring that each member has an opportunity to grow and develop as a result of this experience.

Our Response

As a result of this finding, Iowa Reading Corps will explore options to incorporate more targeted opportunities for members to experience an even higher level of growth and development throughout their term of service. Specific ideas include:

- Formalizing the structure for members to develop personal and professional goals at the beginning of their term of service, to revisit those goals at the mid-way point of their term of service and to then evaluate their progress at the end of the program year.
- Provide testimonials from AmeriCorps alums at the beginning of the year so members begin to internalize how service can strengthen their personal and professional skills.
- Provide opportunities for members to "check-in" or network with one another on a regular basis to discuss personal and professional growth and to provide feedback to program staff.

Finding 3: Lack of AmeriCorps Identity

Description

As a statewide program, Iowa Reading Corps AmeriCorps members are often the only AmeriCorps member serving in their assigned elementary school and are sometimes the only AmeriCorps member serving in the community. While some areas of the state, including Story County, Sioux City and the Quad Cities, host a cohort of 4-10 Iowa Reading Corps AmeriCorps members, most members only see one another, in person, for three training sessions concentrated at the beginning of their term of service and an end of year celebration. In an attempt to provide more opportunities for members to connect with one another, Iowa Reading Corps AmeriCorps members also participate in monthly, web-based trainings that include structured opportunities for facilitated networking and resource sharing.

While the web-based trainings provide a bridge to help members stay connected after the initial, in-person trainings, it became apparent throughout the Seeing Impact Project interviews that members form a stronger connection to their school and local community throughout their term of service than to AmeriCorps. Specifically, members identified a stronger connection with their Reading Corps school than with the AmeriCorps program. Due to the structure of our statewide program, this was a disheartening, but not necessarily surprising, finding. Throughout the past two years, program staff members have worked to implement more targeted strategies for fostering the spirit of AmeriCorps service amongst members who serve in communities that are often hours apart from one another, but this project has clarified the need to strengthen this component of our program. To highlight, when members were asked to reflect upon connections formed throughout their term of service, we expected to hear members describe connections that they had made with other AmeriCorps members or with the AmeriCorps program in general. However, members focused upon connections with the school and community:

> "I was surprised by how connected I got with my school. I knew I would connect with the kids because I was working with them one-on-one every day, but I also connected with the school and staff. The staff really made me feel like I was part of the team and I felt really comfortable talking to everyone. I thought more of the connection would be with the students, but I felt so connected to everyone at my school." (Female, Iowa Reading Corps alumni)

> "I felt like I was really part of something at my school this year. At first, I thought I would just be this volunteer in the school. Now, I feel like I'm really part of the school and everyone has been so supportive. The relationships I've made at my school have exceeded my expectations and were even more positive than I thought they would be when I first signed up for this position." (Female, first-year member)

> "Getting to know the staff and faculty at my school has been so exciting. I went into this thinking that I would be on my own, but that hasn't been the case at all. Other teachers have been

really interested in the program and what we're doing. It's those connections with the school, kids and staff that made the difference for me." (Female, first-year member)

Significance

While members seemed to understand AmeriCorps as a program, they didn't form a strong identity as an AmeriCorps member throughout their term of service. This is significant because we hope our current AmeriCorps members will become alumni who advocate for national service and share their stories of service to recruit future AmeriCorps members. However, without forming a strong bond or connection with AmeriCorps, it is unlikely that members will stay engaged in issues facing the national service field after they have exited from their term of service. While Iowa Reading Corps wants our members to form strong connections with their Reading Corps schools and community, we also need to strive to ensure that members form a connection to AmeriCorps and their fellow members.

Our Response

As Iowa Reading Corps continues to expand to serve more rural school districts across the state, there will likely be at least a few members each year who are the only AmeriCorps members serving in their communities. However, other areas of the state will see a continued expansion in the number of members serving within larger districts. For these reasons, we will explore the following options to strengthen the AmeriCorps identity among members serving independently or within a larger cohort:

- Schedule regional meet-ups for AmeriCorps members that allow face-to-face networking and resource sharing.

- Create social media groups, featuring content facilitated by second-year members, to provide another platform for members to use technology to connect.

- Create an informal mentoring program for Iowa Reading Corps AmeriCorps Alums and new members to strengthen their AmeriCorps identity.

Finding 4: Uncovering a Sense of Community

Description

Iowa Reading Corps AmeriCorps members serve in one elementary school throughout the duration of their term of service. While some members serve in a familiar community (perhaps where they grew up or attended college), other members relocate to complete their term of service in an entirely new community. By serving the same community for eleven months, members are offered a unique glimpse into the needs of their community and an opportunity to get engaged outside of the school setting. For example, many members collaborate with community-based organizations, such as local United Ways or youth-based nonprofits, to recruit volunteers for service projects and/or to earn additional, literacy-based AmeriCorps service hours during school breaks. These opportunities seemed to positively impact members' AmeriCorps experiences by fostering a sense of belonging and new or renewed sense of community engagement:

"This experience has changed my connection to this community because I've seen a side of the community that I didn't think too much about before this year. I grew up on a different side of the community – on this side of town many families have a lot more struggles. It's given me more of a connection to people who I might not have associated with before this experience. There are things going on in my own community that I wasn't aware of at all." (Female, first-year member)

"This year has been a pretty massive change from being a college student, which feels like only a temporary attachment to a community, to making this commitment. Saying that I live here, that I'm part of this community – feeling a sense of connection and permanence has changed and improved how I see my community. I sometimes feel like I live in a different city than my college friends. Interacting with families, parents, kids – it changes your whole perception. Having that range of interaction with different people – which is not at all what you experience in college." (Female, first-year member)

"I've really learned how to get involved in my community. Not just with my students, but with teachers, families and different organizations. Now I have a better sense of community awareness – I felt like I lived in a bubble before AmeriCorps. I've been doing things this year in the community that I never thought about doing a year ago." (Female, first-year member)

In addition, on the quantitative, end-of-year survey, 12 of the 22 Iowa Reading Corps AmeriCorps members strongly agreed that they felt committed to seek opportunities to volunteer in school settings following their term of AmeriCorps service. An additional 7 members agreed with the above statement. Furthermore, 21 of the 22 members agreed that they felt committed to continued community service and 100% of members would encourage others to serve as an AmeriCorps member with the program.

Significance

This finding is significant because it demonstrates the positive impact of community engagement throughout Iowa Reading Corps AmeriCorps members' term of service. While members spend the majority of their service hours providing one-on-one tutoring in their Reading Corps schools, these reflections highlight the benefit of including opportunities for members to engage in the larger community throughout their term of service to build connections outside of the school setting. While all AmeriCorps programs in Iowa are required to include a volunteer engagement component in their members' service contracts, most Reading Corps programs (located across the nation), do not include this requirement. This research solidifies the value of not only incorporating elements of volunteer generation, but of intentionally structuring and continuing to strengthen this component of our program.

Our Response

To strengthen the volunteer generation component of our AmeriCorps program, we will explore the following options:

- Embed service projects and volunteer engagement requirements into members' service experience from the very beginning of their term of service to ensure members understand the importance and benefits of engaging in the larger community.

- Provide training for members to help them refine and develop their leadership and communication skills to boost their confidence and provide a foundation for building relationships.

- Ensure members understand the connection between volunteer generation and community engagement and see the value in the inclusion of this component in an elementary literacy program.

Finding #5: Moving Outside the Bubble

Description

As described in the previous finding, we were pleasantly surprised to hear the sense of belonging and engagement that members experienced in their local communities throughout their term of service. For members who reported especially high levels of community engagement, it is interesting to note that these members were also more likely to note the "ripple effect" of their AmeriCorps service. Specifically, these members highlighted the positive impact that they not only had on their Reading Corps school or students, but the impact that they also had on the larger community:

"Seeing how dedicated everyone in this community is to making a difference for kids and how motivated they are to make the community better has been pretty awesome. It's exciting to see that other people are excited about what you're doing. It's been great to have that interaction on the broader level – seeing the community get involved and feeling the enthusiasm of others has made me feel like I'm connected and making a difference in the community on a much broader sense." (Female, first-year member)

"Bridging the gap between the school and community has been a pretty big accomplishment for me. It makes me want to keep the ball rolling to keep volunteering and making connections in my community. AmeriCorps sort of lit a fire in me to even want to make a difference and to really believe that I can make a difference." (Male, first-year member)

"We had a family night at school and I just couldn't believe the number of teachers and parents who came and showed up to help for just half an hour. I had never witnessed that may people coming out and helping others before. I had 39 volunteers that night – it really affirmed that there are people who care – teachers, parents, etc. out there who want to help make a difference for kids." (Female, first-year member)

These members seemed to have developed an understanding of the role that community volunteers and organizations can play in supporting academic achievement and youth development. However, this experience was not universal for all of our AmeriCorps members. Some members had a more difficult time forming connections to their community and also faced more initial challenges getting engaged. While it was discouraging to hear that some members struggled to get engaged in the community, it seemed particularly significant that these members persevered and still seemed to internalize the value of community engagement:

"There really didn't seem to be a lot of programs here to volunteer with. The opportunities that I did find were during times that didn't work for me and might not work for a lot of families either. My coach and I looked at every single option within the community and finally found a few that were focused on my AmeriCorps service. The lack of participation from parents at our family literacy night was a bummer, but also made me want to try and get more people involved." (Female, first-year member)

"Our community doesn't really have a lot of opportunities to post volunteer projects or find other ways to get involved. I couldn't really find anything online, so I started talking to people Partnering with the middle school and high school was the most helpful. The principals were so excited to have their students volunteer at the elementary school and get more involved with the younger students." (Female, first-year member)

"I was surprised by the lack of advertised volunteer opportunities that are put out there for people who are trying to find a way to get more involved. It's been hard for me to find things outside of the school to participate in. I have to really dig to find opportunities and sometimes there are none to be found in the community." (Female, first-year member)

Significance

This finding is significant because it not only demonstrates the positive impact of community engagement on a member's service experience, but also highlights the need for members to draw upon their own internal motivations if they experience challenges or bumps in the road as they attempt to build connections within the community. For members who do not have this particular drive, it will also be important for staff to be prepared to support these members by facilitating connections to local United Ways or encouraging site supervisors to help identify ways that members can further engage in the community and build lasting relationships.

The duality of these findings is also reflected in the quantitative survey responses. While 63.6% of members strongly agreed that felt committed to ongoing community service, 31.8% of members agreed with the statement and 4.5% stated no opinion. Ideally, we hope that 100% of members would exit from service with a commitment to ongoing community service.

Our Response

While each member who participated in the SIP interview reported at least a small increase in community engagement throughout their term of service, the members who seemed to have the most positive experiences were those who went above and beyond to engage in their community outside of the school setting. For some of these members, personal motivation likely played a significant role. For others, particularly those who serve in communities that embrace volunteerism and foster a culture of service, the sense of belongingness might have occurred more organically. For these reasons, we will explore the following options to ensure that all members develop a stronger sense of connection and belongingness in their community throughout their term of service:

- Provide training and resources for site supervisors to serve as "facilitators" to help members find opportunities to engage in the community.
- Create structured projects for members to "jump start" community connections. For example, members might interview leaders from local businesses, religious institutions and/or nonprofits to learn more about community organizations while also sharing more information about AmeriCorps.
- Incorporate more opportunities for members to reflect on community engagement.

Finding #6: Crafting a Lifetime of Service

Description

One of the goals of national service programs is to provide AmeriCorps members with an intensive service experience that not only promotes increased community engagement, but hopefully sparks an ongoing commitment to volunteerism and civic engagement. Throughout the duration of the SIP interviews, we were excited to hear that each member expressed a commitment to staying civically engaged as community volunteers following their term of AmeriCorps service. Interestingly, while all members expressed a desire to stay actively engaged in their communities following their term of service, some members expressed a more deep and enduring commitment to volunteerism and community engagement than others. However, even members who expressed only a surface-level commitment to volunteerism still seemed to internalize the positive impact and importance of volunteerism. Additionally, members also reported that they felt better equipped to independently research and participate in future volunteer opportunities. In summary, members not only internalized (at varying degrees) the importance of volunteerism, they also experienced an increased awareness of opportunities to volunteer in their local community.

"This has opened up a lot of doors to the community that maybe I wasn't able to see before. In college, I thought I would love to do some volunteer work, but I had no idea how to get involved or where to start looking for opportunities. Now I have better resources and I know where to look. Now I want to be a stable force for change in the community and with these kids. I'm definitely more committed." (Female, first-year member)

"As a community member, I'm going to be a much more intentional volunteer. There's a lot more places I know about now and I have more confidence in myself. Now, I would feel confident taking on leadership roles as a volunteer. I wouldn't have tried to do that before on my own – I've always worked within an agency or program that already exists." (Female, second-year member)

"I know I will continue volunteering and getting involved after AmeriCorps. Once you've had your eyes opened to things, it's hard to turn away at that point. For me, the difficult part is actually taking that step to get involved or start volunteering. Just going by myself to volunteer with a new group was a huge step for me this year. Now I don't have that anxiety and I know it's not about me, it's about what I can offer to someone else." (Female, first-year member)

Significance

This finding is significant because our goal is to not only provide opportunities for AmeriCorps members to develop leadership and professional skills, but to set the stage for a lifetime of service. By encouraging members to further engage in their community, through literacy-based activities or summer enrichment programs, they become more aware of how they can continue to serve their community following the end of their term of service. Furthermore, one of the first steps in becoming civically engaged is learning where to look to find volunteer opportunities in the local community. While we suspected that our members would continue volunteering after their AmeriCorps service, this research helps us develop a more complete understanding of how and why members stay civically engaged as alums.

Our Response

While each member described at least a surface-level commitment to volunteerism, we will explore the following options to ensure that each member develops a more deep awareness of civic engagement and expresses a lasting desire to remain engaged following their term of service:

- Incorporate more specific options/ideas for members to stay civically engaged during the required Life After AmeriCorps Training.
- Include a mini-training during our initial AmeriCorps member orientation regarding how to find a local volunteer opportunity (utilize online search engines, United Way websites, local newspapers, etc.)
- Provide more structured and meaningful opportunities for members to share their stories of service as an alumni.

Conclusion

This evaluation model has provided our team with crucial insight into the experiences of our Iowa Reading Corps AmeriCorps members. While we have previously relied upon quantitative research methods to measure the impact of our program on members, the addition of qualitative research provides a more comprehensive and compelling understanding of member experiences. Furthermore, the qualitative findings not only support our existing quantitative measures, but illuminate new areas of our program model that need to be adjusted to further promote an impactful experience for all members. We believe that these changes and adjustments will not only strengthen our members' experiences in our specific program, but will hopefully spark a fire within each member to embark upon a lifetime of service.

AMERICORPS PARTNERING TO PROTECT CHILDREN, IOWA STATE UNIVERSITY—CHILD WELFARE RESEARCH AND TRAINING PROJECT

Amanda J. McCurley, Janet N. Melby,
Emily J. Jansen, Yuk C. Pang

INTRODUCTION

From February-August 2015, the AmeriCorps Partnering to Protect Children Project Impact team learned and applied an approach to evaluate the effects of placing AmeriCorps members in Community Partnerships to Protect Children (CPPC) host sites. The evaluation process coincided with the first year of our AmeriCorps program which recruited and placed its first AmeriCorps members in October 2014. The evaluation process provided an opportunity to systematically assess the host site supervisors' perceptions regarding the impact AmeriCorps members are having through service in their host communities. This report presents our findings and offers recommendations that are based on interviews and responses to survey questions that we designed to get at the deep and lasting impact of our AmeriCorps program on community progress toward implementing the Community Partnership approach.

Question of Inquiry

Two major questions guided the AmeriCorps Partnering to Protect Children Impact team: (1) What deep and lasting impacts result from AmeriCorps members' service at Community Partnership sites? (2) What modifications in the current AmeriCorps Partnering to Protect Children program are recommended to facilitate progress toward attaining desired outcomes?

AmeriCorps Partnering to Protect Children

The AmeriCorps Partnering to Protect Children (APPC) program is operated through the Child Welfare Research and Training Project (CWRTP) at Iowa State University. An overarching goal of the program is to expand and improve local efforts to prevent child abuse and neglect in underserved rural communities and urban areas with high poverty rates in Iowa. During the first year (2014-2015), eight full-time, two half-time, and one minimum-time AmeriCorps members served nine host sites. These AmeriCorps members collaborated with stakeholders in Communities Partnerships for Protecting Children host sites or DECAT sites throughout Iowa. In addition, two members were based at Iowa State University with the program director and provided statewide outreach. They served with local coordinators to implement culturally informed and locally relevant services and supports. Members were responsible for outreach efforts and presentations to engage community leaders, service providers and families in local children safety efforts. In addition, the members were expected to recruit and involve community volunteers in community service activities.

Community Partnerships to Protect Children

The Community Partnerships for Protecting Children (CPPC / Community Partnership) approach is an evidence-based multi-component strategy of the Iowa Department of Human Services (DHS) to increase community awareness and coordination of services to reduce abuse and neglect of children. Currently, 40 Partnership sites operate in Iowa, some serving multi-county areas. This community-based approach to protective assessment grew from initial work in Cedar Rapids in 1995 and now encompasses the entire state. Fundamental to the Community Partnership approach is the development and implementation of four core complementary strategies: (1) Community Partnership Involvement; (2) Shared Decision Making; (3) Community/Neighborhood Networking; and (4) Individualized Course of Action utilizing family team and youth transition meetings. The Community Partnership Evaluation developed by DHS is the primary tool used to assess site progress in the four key strategies. The evaluation tool is a multi-component self-assessment survey that sites complete each year as required for participation in and receipt of IDHS funding for their Partnership program. Communities report their progress along the four-level engagement continuum: (1) Awareness, (2) Planning, (3) Implementation, and finally (4) Sustainability. Within the framework of the self-assessment, each site is responsible for assessing and developing a plan to address local needs.

Child Welfare Research and Training Project

The Child Welfare Research and Training Project (CWRTP) at Iowa State University (ISU) has had a contractual partnership with the Iowa Department of Human Services (DHS) since 1989. As part of an annually renewed contract with the Iowa Department of Human Services, CWRTP has delivered training, outreach and evaluation services to DHS services workers and contracted providers. Contract staff include a specialist position who facilitates implementation of community partnership and associated initiatives in active collaboration and partnership with the Iowa Department of Human Services, specifically for the Division of Adult, Children and Family Services. The work is completed in close consultation with the Iowa DHS. Special focus is on field-related work with community partners throughout the state and creation of written materials, including direct training and facilitation (e.g., Family Team Decision Making, Building a Better Future, Transitioning Youth, assisting in coordination of various train-the-trainers, coaching and mentoring for Dream Teams, and participating in steering committee and various work groups).

As part of the state fiscal year 2015 Service Training Contract, the Iowa DHS provided the required match to support the creation and implementation of the AmeriCorps Partnering to Protect Children program which was begun September 1, 2014. DHS state funds provided the required match for financial support received from the National Corporation for Community Services awarded to Iowa State University thorough the Iowa Commission on Volunteer Service.

Linking AmeriCorps Members with Community Partnerships

Local Community Partnership sites apply to host an AmeriCorps member and are the primary source for recruiting potential AmeriCorps members from the communities in which programs operate. The AmeriCorps members are supervised by local host site supervisors who are responsible for guiding and mentoring members on a day-to-day basis. Both the AmeriCorps members and their host site supervisors have regular contact with the full-time AmeriCorps program director, Amanda McCurley. She coordinates the AmeriCorps program conjunction with the goals and objectives of the Community Partnership approach and in communication with the DHS and the ISU specialist responsible for implementing the partnership initiative throughout Iowa.

METHODOLOGY

Over a period of two months the project team administered two evaluation instruments (qualitative telephone interview and quantitative online survey) they developed for the impact project. Participants were invited by email to respond to an approximately 45 minute telephone interview that was conducted by one of three impact project team members (Amanda McCurley, Yuk Pang, and Emily Jansen). The twelve questions asked about and probed for deeper insights into the impact of the AmeriCorps member in bringing about desire changes at the Community Partnership. Next, all participants were invited by email to complete an online survey administered using the Qualtrics survey tool. The survey included 19 questions coded from low to high, for example, 1= never (or not at all) to 5 = always (or strongly agree) and four open-ended questions that asked the respondent to assess the situation at the local host site before vs. after involvement of the AmeriCorps member. Both instruments included questions about the attitudes toward and involvement of families, service providers, and people in the community with the Community Partnership.

Invited participants were nine host site supervisors of AmeriCorps Partnering to Protect Children members during the current program year (2014-2015), who did not participate on the impact project team, or the administration of the interviews and surveys. These included coordinators of the eight Community Partnerships to Protect Children (CPPC) and DECAT sites, as well as one university staff supervising a part-time AmeriCorps member engaged with Community Partnerships statewide. Of those invited, all nine participated in the telephone interviews. Eight of the nine invited host site supervisors (89%) responded to the online survey.

Dr. Steve Patty oversaw the learning and the execution of the impact project approach. He is considered an expert in the field of qualitative assessment and organizational change. The project was reviewed and determined to be exempt from Institutional Review Board oversight by Iowa State University prior to data collection.

FINDINGS

Although CWRTP has been involved with the Community Partnership program for several years, this is CWRTP's first year to administer an AmeriCorps program through which AmeriCorps members are placed at local Community Partnership sites throughout the state. It is essential that we evaluate the impact of the AmeriCorps members as perceived by their local host site supervisors.

As a result of analyzing the data obtained from host site supervisors, the impact project team identified a number of themes that warrant consideration to move the AmeriCorps Partnering to Protect Children vision forward. This report examines the following themes:

Finding 1   Successful collaboration requires member initiative and host site supervisor mentoring.

Finding 2   Innovation depends on assessing and using resources to achieve goals.

Finding 3   Embracing an AmeriCorps identity and role aids progress toward desired outcomes.

Finding 4   It takes a community to better protect, support, an strengthen vulnerable children and families.

Finding 5   AmeriCorps member strengths are a foundation from which they can generate impact.

Finding 6   Sharing insight, strategies, and tools expands site capacity to achieve goals.

Finding 7   Commitment to the Community Partnership philosophy generates enduring results.

Finding 8   A diverse network boosts site capacity to reach goals.

Finding #1: Fusing AmeriCorps member initiative with Community Partnership host site supervisor mentoring establishes a firm foundation for successful collaboration.

Overview

A theme from the interviews with AmeriCorps host site supervisors is that the strengths of the AmeriCorps member provide a foundation from which they generate impact. However, member strengths need coordination and nurturing to boost their impact and meet host site and program goals. Fusing an AmeriCorps member's strengths with a site supervisor's mentoring and guidance is an effective way to achieve the impacts that host site supervisors envision for their communities.

Description

A. AmeriCorps members benefit from supportive guidance. The data show that AmeriCorps members can have many strengths and characteristics, yet their initiative and effectiveness can waver or be misdirected without constructive and focused guidance. "...APPC members' excitement and compassion in their work also play important roles in community networking." The APPC program expects the host site supervisors to provide collaboration, guidance, and positive reinforcement for AmeriCorps members. Interviewees spoke frequently about AmeriCorps member strengths such as versatility, work-ethic, dedication, passion, empathy, experience, and personal character and values. When qualities are lacking, the local partnership site can suffer.

Another interviewee described to the AmeriCorps member's tenacity and dedication and how the AmeriCorps member "reminds [service providers] of their responsibilities." This host site supervisor meets with the AmeriCorps member for supervision once a week. Supervision between the host site supervisor and AmeriCorps member allows a structured time to meet and check-in with one another and to discuss goals, future plans, strengths, areas of improvements, and other observations the host site supervisor and AmeriCorps member may have. Scheduled supervision time creates opportunities for supportive guidance throughout the AmeriCorps members' term of service.

Another site supervisor stated, "I really trust both of [the AmeriCorps members] and it has made my life much easier." This site supervisor described the benefit of combining a "coordinator that cares" with AmeriCorps members who have the competency to recruit and involve local community agencies and volunteers. Several interviewees mentioned having compassion for their AmeriCorps members, and described a close relationship with the member. The quantitative survey data indicated that host supervisors perceived an increase in consistent participation by service providers in the Community Partnership from before to after AmeriCorps member involvement; on a scale from 1 (never) to 5 (all the time), the average increased from 3.38 to 3.75.

Most interviewees appreciate their AmeriCorps member's excitement and compassion; however, a few expressed disappointment in the member's perceived inability to achieve the "great things" the host site supervisors have seen "come out of AmeriCorps in the past". For instance, one interviewee said that the member was helpful at first, and service providers were relieved to have help, but an AmeriCorps member's lack of follow-through [on commitments] later on discouraged other providers and eventually "was more of a hassle than it was worth and they [service providers] had a bad experience."

B. **AmeriCorps members bring unique strengths to host sites.** AmeriCorps members were sometimes valued for their distinct skills and backgrounds by the host site supervisors we interviewed. For example, when asked about member impact, a host site supervisor enthusiastically described how the member was approachable for parents due to her age and experience as a parent. "My member, she's a non-traditional [in terms of age] member--she has teenage kids. [Parents] really look at her as more of the expert. Trust her more." Another laughed slightly as she explained how her APPC member used her organizational skills and creativity to increase the quality of promotional items, commenting, "[The newsletter] was much better than what I came up with!"

C. Host site supervisors who are AmeriCorps alums bring specific expectations. A couple of the interviewees acknowledged that being an AmeriCorps alum shaped their perception and expectations of AmeriCorps member impact. One site supervisor stated that the AmeriCorps program "does take a special kind of person" who has the motivation to show commitment despite receiving a monthly stipend "no matter what." Another alum cited the APPC member as "increasing" awareness and networking with previously untapped faith-based community.

D. Collaborative involvement of supervisors and members provides a model for community partnership collaboration. The interview data show that joint involvement of host site supervisors and AmeriCorps members in Community Partnership activities and outreach helps to increase impact. Some host site supervisors appear to be leaving the community outreach component solely to the AmeriCorps members. The online survey results showed an increase in community members' engagement with Community Partnerships when comparing its rating for before with after AmeriCorps' involvement; on a scale from 1 to 5, the average increased from 2.5 to 3.5. In the interviews, some host site supervisors tended to describe what the "member did" versus what "we did." In contrast, one interviewee who described a "close relationship" with the AmeriCorps member mentioned joint involvement in activities and "seeing" what the member does to support community members even after they leave an activity. This host site supervisor placed heavy emphasis on advocacy, collaboration, and holistic approaches to networking.

Significance

In general, the host site supervisors expect their AmeriCorps members to take the initiative to support their host sites. However, it remains unclear whether site supervisors are embracing the opportunity to help the AmeriCorps members to apply and grow their strengths to create a platform of collaborative effort. Doing outreach activities together could provide opportunities for mentoring and model collaborative partnerships. In turn, this may increase the willingness of community people to join Community Partnership host sites. Outreach is a method to overcome a lack of community investment and support for child abuse prevention. It is clear that both AmeriCorps member taking initiative and host site supervisor mentoring and guidance contribute to building a firm foundation for program success.

Our Response

- Clarify an expectation for host site supervisors to mentor AmeriCorps members during recruitment and matching.

- Assess strengths of AmeriCorps members before, during, and after their service to find what influences their initiative-taking over time.

- Emphasize the mentoring role of host site supervisors during their orientation/training.

- Provide a member-orientation checklist for host site supervisors.

- Encourage host site supervisors to review and plan for collaborative engagement by becoming familiar with and reviewing the reporting tool AmeriCorps members fill-out and submit to the program director on a monthly basis.

Finding #2: Innovation in Community Partnerships benefits from assessing resources and using them to achieve goals.

Overview

A key theme that emerged was that innovations and progress toward reaching Community Partnership goals is facilitated when sites identify and use available resources to achieve goals. The data revealed that this can be difficult for some host site supervisors and AmeriCorps members who have a limited vision regarding the resources and opportunities. These host site supervisors mentioned having little time to make connections and said that local funding cuts and policy changes have had negative impacts on local programs. Host sites where AmeriCorps members and site supervisors are willing and able to think outside the box and to take appropriate risks were able to introduce fresh activities and approaches to achieve site goals, often through the assistance of their AmeriCorps members. This involved identifying a need, thinking broadly about available resources, and then being innovative in the use of resources to meet that need.

Description

A. **Being stuck in crisis mode inhibits creativity and innovation.** One site supervisor who articulated a focus on limitations during the interview said, "…AmeriCorps could increase our access to families…we are still stuck in raising awareness and getting everyone on board…and that is the level I am at because it is what I have time for…the more we can be out in the community and making connections with families, progress will happen faster…" Similarly, several other site supervisors mentioned that the majority of their time is spent focusing on immediate needs (i.e., crisis mode) which limits their site's time to focus on building prevention strategies.

B. **Community Partnerships benefit from openness to new approaches.** Other site supervisors expressed a wider perspective. For example, a site supervisor stated, "Long distance connections have been opened by the member and the opportunity to collaborate with a coordinator in [nearby location] which never happened before." The survey data indicate that host supervisors perceive service providers to be more aware of other service providers as a result of AmeriCorps involvement; on a scale from 1 (not at all aware) to 5 (extremely aware), the average increased from 3.25 to 3.75. A few supervisors noted that AmeriCorps members' interactions with families helped build relationships and identify information [needs]. These interactions can lead to improved collaboration and communication between agencies and among community people. One interviewee stated that trusting an AmeriCorps member to use creativity and resourcefulness helped to ease the host site supervisor's stress and resulted in the Community Partnership site's advisory board agreeing to join additional projects proposed by the AmeriCorps member.

Significance

Many of the host sites and communities have limited resources (including time, money, and expertise). It is important that host site leadership and AmeriCorps members see beyond the immediate crisis or situation to identify existing resources to empower families and build community connections (often through small steps) in order to achieve the long-term goal of preventing child abuse. Along with assessing community needs and identifying resources, for successful implementation of new and innovative approaches it is important to establish and maintain trust between and among the host site supervisor, AmeriCorps member, advisory board, service agencies, families, and others in the community.

Our Response

- Train AmeriCorps members in the principles and techniques of asset-mapping.
- Emphasize key components and strategies that help to lay the groundwork for building trusting professional working relationships.

- Provide opportunities for AmeriCorps members and host site supervisors to share stories about appropriate innovations and risk-taking.

Finding #3: Embracing an AmeriCorps identity and role is the launch pad for Community Partnership progress.

Overview

An important theme that emerged during analysis was the emphasis placed on the members' AmeriCorps identity and role, and how this can impact (both positively and negatively) their host site and community. For this theme, the host site supervisor discussed AmeriCorps member knowledge about Community Partnerships, the community's perception of the AmeriCorps member, member connectedness to other AmeriCorps members, and member role confusion (both by site supervisor and AmeriCorps member).

Description

There are many elements that contribute to and make up the AmeriCorps member identity and role. In order for a member to positively impact their service site and community, he or she must embrace their AmeriCorps role and use it as a launching pad into progress toward providing support for achieving community goals. The following elements were the most common in the interviewee responses.

A. **Community perceptions of the AmeriCorps members are mixed.** The data show that AmeriCorps members are seen as role-models in their communities. AmeriCorps members who serve directly with vulnerable children and families can connect them to resources they need, and also instill trust and investment in the Community Partnership, local service providers, and other people in the community. One site supervisor commented that through the AmeriCorps member's service, families became aware that they have a voice and are connected to resources to meet their needs. The impact of trust may be reflected in quantitative survey results related to how well

CPPC is received by community members before versus after AmeriCorps involvement.

On the reverse side, the data show that the AmeriCorps program reputation suffers when an AmeriCorps member does not live up to their service expectations and is not committed to AmeriCorps, their program, or the Community Partnership. Since Community Partnership host sites require the AmeriCorps member to interact with the community on a regular basis, their interactions (both positive and negative) leave a lasting impact. In addition, Community Partnership host sites that do not promote AmeriCorps hinder the reinforcement of the member's AmeriCorps identity.

B. **AmeriCorps member connectedness with other AmeriCorps members helps to strengthen their impact.** Another way to reinforce the AmeriCorps program and member identity is through members being connected with each other. A few host site supervisors acknowledged collaborations among members can build AmeriCorps pride and identity and strengthen bonds between Community Partnership sites across Iowa. This type of information sharing among AmeriCorps members could strengthen efforts to prevent child abuse and neglect across Iowa. AmeriCorps members who collaborate with each other could improve host site decision-making processes, strengthen their ability to evaluate successes and failures, and identify adjustments to improve future community-based prevention efforts. In response to the online survey, one host site supervisor wrote, "My AmeriCorps member has been very helpful and has had many important opportunities on a statewide level."

C. **Confusion about the AmeriCorps member's role can inhibit program success.** The impact of AmeriCorps members may be constrained by role confusion on the part of the member and/or the site supervisor. Some site supervisors struggled to explain the role of the AmeriCorps member or to give suggestions for improvement, perhaps because of a lack of understanding of AmeriCorps and the Community Partnership approach. A full and solid understanding of AmeriCorps and member roles and program expectations by the site supervisor is key to a successful service term.

When both the AmeriCorps member and Community Partnership host site supervisor are on the same page and fully understand the AmeriCorps identity and expectations, the member role can be reinforced and become an asset to the host site. Descriptive data from the quantitative survey indicates a slight increase in favorable attitude toward service providers from families from before to after AmeriCorps involvement. Being new to the supervisor role was "easier" for one interviewee who explained that having an AmeriCorps member who understood AmeriCorps and Community Partnerships gave the host site supervisor the feeling that members "know what they are talking about," and could fill many different roles to adapt to "whatever the group [local site] needs."

Significance

AmeriCorps members and supervisors who fully understand and embrace the AmeriCorps roles can launch themselves towards progress in their communities. An over-arching goal of the Community Partnership initiative is for local sites to address community needs, which are difficult to assess without the trust, feedback, and investment of people in the community. AmeriCorps members and host site supervisors can increase trust by helping local communities understand what AmeriCorps members do and the AmeriCorps member role in assisting host sites to implement the Community Partnership approach. In addition, AmeriCorps members can support one another across the state of Iowa and instill a sense of pride in the AmeriCorps program by collaborating amongst themselves on a more personal level. This support could also increase communication between Community Partnership site supervisors and create a broader Iowa Community Partnership network. AmeriCorps members working together from different partnership sites, can help bridge the gap and dissolve the silo effect that currently exists between the Community Partnership sites throughout the state of Iowa.

Our Response

- Thoroughly screen potential AmeriCorps members during recruitment to find those who are committed and dedicated to the AmeriCorps mission and the philosophy of Community Partnerships to Protect Children.
- Mandate in-depth, extensive trainings for paired AmeriCorps members and Community Partnership site supervisors to AmeriCorps and Community Partnerships, will help both the AmeriCorps member and site supervisor be more impactful at their host site and community,
- Provide access to continuing education, training and support to the AmeriCorps member on a regular and on-going basis.
- Plan opportunities for AmeriCorps members to travel across Iowa to interact and collaborate to reinforce AmeriCorps identity and a sense of belonging to the AmeriCorps program.

Finding #4: It takes a community.

Overview

Another important theme is that it takes a community to better protect, support, and strengthen vulnerable children and families instead of relying solely on Community Partnership supervisors. The AmeriCorps members can help to overcome obstacles and build networking through their expected role tasks and responsibilities, as well as their dedication to serve the community. One role for AmeriCorps members is to establish close partnerships with their assigned local Community Partnership host sites and to assist efforts for the prevention of child abuse through awareness and collaboration with people in the community and volunteers. Another role is to collaborate with local sites to strengthen community linkages and to provide service providers and community people with information about risk factors and supports needed by vulnerable children and families.

Description

The interviews with host site supervisors highlighted that as a result of AmeriCorps member involvement, the local Community Partnership host sites were able to identify obstacles and needs to serve children and families in the community. The obstacles mentioned included limited local resources, site supervisors with a heavy workload, pre-existing attitudes, and history of the community, etc. These obstacles can prevent service providers and others in the community from actively engaging in serving children and families in their communities.

A. **Sharing the workload broadens the impact.** During the interview, one of the Community Partnership host site supervisors talked about how AmeriCorps members helped to identify gaps in resources and ways to incorporate this information into their decision-making and collaboration to fill those gaps, then continue to identify other community needs. Another interviewee stated the AmeriCorps member "...helps people pinpoint what needs to be done and figures out how to do it...the member will figure out who can help you." Community Partnership host sites showed appreciation for having more than one person to do community outreach, easing the supervisor's workload in leadership as the AmeriCorps member shares responsibility for educating and engaging people in the community to actively serve children and families in their communities.

B. **Commitment to the Community Partnership approach increases impact.** Our data show that AmeriCorps members are directly serving their host communities by connecting people to resources and parenting programs, hosting outreach events, and indirectly by maintaining social media resources and creating resource guides or promotional fliers. Site supervisors valued that AmeriCorps members provide a role model for how to network and motivate community people, specifically service providers. A site supervisor said, "...when they see someone encouraging them to keep doing what they are doing, that's helpful." In their responses to the online survey, host site supervisors reported that the community engagement in the local Community Partnership, assessed on a scale from 1 (not at all) to 5 (extremely engaged), increased from 2.5 to 3.5 as a result of AmeriCorps member involvement.

Significance

AmeriCorps members help to bring service providers and people in the community together. This also provides support for local Community Partnership host sites efforts to reach their goals through the initiative's four core strategies (i.e., shared decision-making, neighborhood networking, individualized course of action, and practice change). As communities build resources from increased awareness and networking, the whole community can develop sustainability within host site leadership and facilitate a paradigm shift. The responses of Community Partnership site supervisors reflect a theme of appreciation and relief from having support from AmeriCorps members that undertake outreach activities that raise awareness in the community.

Our Response

- Encourage AmeriCorps members to engage in neighborhood networking through outreach to community groups beyond agencies and service providers.
- Potentially arrange opportunities for the general public to learn more about Community Partnerships and current outreach activities in the community.

Finding #5: Strengths of an AmeriCorps member build a foundation from which they can generate impact.

Overview

AmeriCorps members bring a diversity of backgrounds and skills to their service at Community Partnership host sites. The data show that certain AmeriCorps member characteristics can positively influence their experiences and accomplishments (e.g., initiative taking, previous work experiences, commitment, etc.). At the same time, certain Community Partnership host site characteristics can expand and enhance members' impact (e.g., clear expectations, access to programs and trainings, opportunities to interact with families, site-specific projects, occasions to engage with the community, openness to trying something new, etc.).

Description

A. **AmeriCorps member knowledge of and commitment to the Community Partnership approach provides a foundation for impact.** Competent and knowledgeable AmeriCorps members help expand the investment of Community Partnership host site supervisors. Site supervisors greatly benefit from AmeriCorps members who are self-aware and have prior knowledge of the Community Partnership approach. One interviewee stated that it is encouraging to see more opportunities for outreach, more direct connections built, and increases in community knowledge of Community Partnerships through the AmeriCorps member's efforts.

The majority of site supervisors provided positive examples of member impact. One site supervisor noted that an AmeriCorps member who has a solid understanding of the Community Partnership approach can have a foundation for building both immediate and lasting impacts. Examples include organizing professional development training so service providers can better serve families and providing linkages between people in the community and service opportunities.

B. **Strengths of an AmeriCorps member influence their impact on Community Partnerships.** When asked, "What has your [AmeriCorps] member done to help identify or increase community awareness of gaps in resources?" many interviewees provided detail about activities of the AmeriCorps member yet were vague or unsure when asked for specific indicators of change in the community. Commitment, empathy, versatility, flexibility, adaptability, maturity, insight, work ethic, dedication, self-awareness, awareness of community needs, and cultural competence were frequently mentioned strengths. For instance, interviewees referenced adaptability as AmeriCorps members being in "...many different roles; your expertise can be whatever the group needs." Others valued AmeriCorps members that were "very active," doing "hard work" or "a lot of work". Others spoke more on AmeriCorps members who were creative with social media and able engage the community. One AmeriCorps member was "developing" Facebook, "revamped our newsletter" and made both more "visually attractive."

When asked about change in community awareness and use of supports and resources, interviewees tended to offer vague answers such as, "I don't have any stories or specifics that indicate a whole lot of change" and "I'm not sure, not right now...." Another example reflected AmeriCorps members' impact on service providers, "I guess I don't know if having a member has changed their [service providers] thinking." These responses show that site supervisors recognize that AmeriCorps members bring strengths to host sites to set the foundation for impact, yet they appear unable to offer specific examples of the community impact made solely by the AmeriCorps members. In their responses to the online survey, host site supervisors reported that the community awareness of resources for vulnerable children and families, measured on a scale from 1 (not at all aware) to 5 (extremely aware), increased from 3.15 to 3.63 as a result of AmeriCorps member involvement.

One explanation for the vague answers could be the length the AmeriCorps members typically serves, which is one year. For example, some interviewees hesitated when talking about incorporating AmeriCorps members into their future visions for their host site saying, "...when you do have long-term ambitions without proper support, you settle for short-term. We try to keep our minds open to long and short-term," therefore it is difficult for host sites to envision long-term goals for AmeriCorps members.

Significance

This finding highlights that AmeriCorps members' strengths impact the Community Partnership host site. Site supervisors vary in their recognition of the inter-connection between member activities and observable short and long-term community changes. Vague answers reveal a lack of communication between site supervisors and AmeriCorps members about long-term impact. This also relates to a limitation of the study design in that we interviewed only site supervisors for their perspectives, and did not include AmeriCorps members or people from the community. Including a broader sample could provide a more comprehensive picture of specific changes that AmeriCorps members generate in the communities they serve.

Our Response

- Encourage discussions between host site supervisors and AmeriCorps members about how to utilize member strengths as foundations to bring impact to host sites.
- Include information about the Community Partnership approach in AmeriCorps member orientation and trainings.
- Include space on the site application for listing short-term and long-term goals of host sites and AmeriCorps member.
- Encourage host site supervisors to revisit their long-term goals when interacting with new AmeriCorps members.

Finding #6: Sharing insight, strategies, and tools expands site capacity to achieve goals.

Overview

In general, a theme missing from interviewee responses about "what works" for Community Partnership sites is the ability to look outside of one's own site. The practice of sharing ideas to achieve Community Partnership goals has professional and personal benefits for people involved in expanding networks. However, based on interview responses, the pooling of personal insight, strategies and tools from innovative approaches to coordinating and networking appears to be an untapped resource.

Description

A. **Community Partnership competency is valued.** Neighborhood networking and outreach are highly valued by all interviewees, and each mentioned how AmeriCorps members support outreach. However, because most AmeriCorps members first learn about the Community Partnership approach after starting their service term, their ability to support host site supervisors and communities may be impeded if they serve a site that is not well-established.

B. **Community awareness and network expansion is lacking.** When interviewees were asked during their interviews to describe the level of awareness in their community, many were unsure, but felt awareness was still lacking. One mentioned they were waiting for data from community surveys. All demonstrated the understanding that Community Partnership network expansion is a matter of finding needs and connecting people to resources through education, hosting resource fairs, and word-of-mouth (including social media), As one interviewee stated, "A lot [of raising awareness] is through social media,". Another interviewee said, "Just need more people involved." Despite an awareness that more people leads to increased capacity, sharing networking tactics across sites is not yet common practice. There was no mention during the interviews of collaboration among Community Partnership sites.

C. **Experience level of host site supervisors influences the uses of strategies.** Community Partnership experience varies across site supervisor, yet all are tasked with using the four core strategies (i.e., shared decision-making, neighborhood networking, individualized course of action, and policy and practice change in local child abuse prevention initiatives). Newer site supervisors explained they were new to Community Partnership and had difficulty, "gauging dedication of those that were regularly attending partnership meetings." As a new site supervisor, it can be difficult to get investment from service providers to join in activities without having a full understanding of Community Partnerships. Other host site supervisors appeared to be comfortable in their leadership role and the Community Partnership approach. These supervisors framed their answers in a future perspective; they talked about "Reaching out to the rest of the community, beyond service providers."

D. Reluctance to use new tactics can hinder outreach. Some site supervisors mentioned, "We don't carve notches," and, "We will take whatever time we must," when describing how they track results of programs and outreach activities. However, several site supervisors described their primarily focus as providing intervention for children and families in current crisis. Furthermore, not all site supervisors are knowledgeable about marketing strategies. Instead of incorporating promotional activities into their outreach activities, these site supervisors rely more on word-of-mouth.

Significance

Learning to use a new tool (whether for tracking, social media, strategic planning, or online surveys) takes time. If Community Partnership site supervisors and their AmeriCorps members share their knowledge and vouch for specific tools, it could encourage those at other sites to adopt new ways to achieve their goals. Exchanging insight, strategies, and tools that have been successful has the potential to save time and reduce stress. Furthermore, turnover may have less of an impact on sites if new site supervisors have access to shared resources or archival data from previous leadership. AmeriCorps members could utilize proven methods to recruit more efficiently; this would allow them to focus on the "next step" that staff desire after building the foundation of their Community Partnership network.

Our Response

- Encourage the use of technological and other solutions to increase sharing across Community Partnership sites in Iowa as a compliment the desired organic (i.e., word-of-mouth) approach for raising awareness.
- Establish a way for archiving successful projects and accomplishments so this information can be easily accessed by supervisors and members (e.g., shared website).
- Ask site supervisors to come prepared to share resource and networking ideas at regional meetings.
- Share examples of small risks that sites and AmeriCorps members have taken that have led to success in achieving goals.
- Synchronize social media resources between all Iowa Community Partnership sites (i.e., "Follow" on Twitter or "Like" on Facebook).

Finding #7: Commitment to the Community Partnership philosophy generates enduring results.

Overview

Another theme that presented itself during the analysis process was the importance of dispelling the vagueness of the Community Partnership philosophy. Embracing the philosophy begins with a core of basic understanding and grows into emotional investment and "becoming a believer," which generates long-term dedication and in turn, community partnerships that increase the well-being of children and families.

Description

The Community Partnerships to Protect Children approach has many things that work, as well as a few obstacles to overcome. The following elements were most common in the interviewees' responses.

A. **The vagueness of the Community Partnership approach is a double-edged sword.** The Community Partnerships for Protecting Children is an approach and not a program, making its core concepts difficult to comprehend. The Community Partnership core strategies boast flexibility and openness as an asset, but its lack of structure requires extensive outreach and commitment. Recruitment can be a time-consuming process for site supervisors. Because sites thrive on community investment, site progress may be slowed if supervisors and AmeriCorps members are unable to understand or explain the approach.

B. **Getting information out there matters.** To overcome the obstacles created by the inherent vagueness in the Community Partnership approach, interviewees described making future plans for outreach. Community outreach is essential for recruitment and networking with families and service providers. Some interviewees directly attributed an increase in community commitment to a rise in outreach. AmeriCorps members give local Community Partnership sites more time to connect with service agencies and families, and to educate those involved with the partnership. Once people and agencies have the information about community resources and needs, they can provide knowledge and resources to meet the gaps in community services. For the online survey, Community Partnership engagement with families, measured from 1 (not at all engaged) to 5 (extremely engaged), increased from 2.88 to 3.13 after AmeriCorps member involvement. Community Partnership seeking out involvement of service providers increased, measured from 1 (never) to 5 (always), increased from 4.13 to 4.38.

C. **Commitment follows awareness.** Some Community Partnership site supervisors said they feel like their "wheels are spinning" when trying to move out of the initial education and investment phase at their host sites. One interviewee mentioned that having an AmeriCorps member has helped increase access to resources for families, despite feeling as if a lack of time restricted her ability to go beyond raising awareness and recruitment. Having additional support from the AmeriCorps member has alleviated stress and allowed more outreach to the community. The AmeriCorps member can bring more community people to the table and also nurture emotional investment in the Community Partnership approach.

Significance

The Community Partnership approach empowers communities to adapt the approach for their needs. They can decide how to meet their community needs using outreach. When the entire community commits to the Community Partnership, it can achieve long-term results, positive impact, and partnerships. Community Partnership site supervisors require more support and commitment in order to progress. Invested and committed community participants make it possible to achieve bigger visions of the future and achieve enduring results.

Our Response

- Develop an interactive tool to promote the Community Partnership approach (i.e., webinar, video).
- Continue to recruit and educate the community on an ongoing basis.
- Utilize various types of social media to provide outreach.
- Develop a systematic approach to outreach.
- Have AmeriCorps members attend the DHS CPPC 101 and 201 Immersion Training.
- Educate and utilize AmeriCorps members to provide outreach and be a community liaison for the Community Partnership.

Finding #8: A diverse network boosts site capacity to reach goals.

Overview

Lastly, results from the interviews reflected the importance of AmeriCorps members' role in neighborhood networking and outreach in the communities they served to reach host site goals. The outcomes accomplished by AmeriCorps members help to expand current community networking, and in turn, host sites are able to serve more children and families with complex needs.

Description

A. **AmeriCorps members help expand networks.** Community Partnership site supervisors explained that AmeriCorps members often appear approachable for community people and serve as a community liaison. Local service providers often contact AmeriCorps members when seeking resources, which helps them resolve families' needs more quickly and allows families to have a voice in the community. Community awareness spreads to more diverse groups through AmeriCorps members who utilize a variety of outreach methods. Newspapers and more conventional information sources, make it possible to include individuals without Internet access. Some interviewees expressed that AmeriCorps members use their direct interaction with the community to bring information to their site supervisors. Most importantly, they often bring families and service providers together. Through AmeriCorps members' work and their passion to better serve the community, service providers see the value of and become committed to the Community Partnership approach as an ongoing process, and are excited to see AmeriCorps member involved in expanding networking across communities. As a result of involvement of the AmeriCorps members, the online survey respondents on a scale from 1 to 5 reported greater awareness among Service Providers of other providers engaged with the Community Partnership (increased from 3.25 to 3.75), as well as greater participation in the Community Partnership (increased from 3.38 to 3.75).

B. **Resource hubs with a diverse group of service providers can serve complex family needs.** One interviewee described how a second neighborhood hub (i.e., resource center) in the community was opened as a result of a second AmeriCorps members' service participation at her Community Partnership host site. The host site supervisor expressed that the AmeriCorps member had a significant impact and that the second neighborhood hub opened faster than they expected. Upon witnessing the AmeriCorps members' impact, the host site supervisor was encouraged to seek more opportunities to reach potential community participants directly. In addition, communities were able to have more knowledge about Community Partnerships through the members' work on outreach and volunteer recruitment. Such outcome from the neighborhood hubs in the community resonates with the goal and strategies of the Community Partnership approach. In response to the online survey, a supervisor wrote, "[My site] has opened a second neighborhood hub and [the] AmeriCorps member has been very instrumental with the expansion. It has been slow going however much progress is being made."

Significance

A diverse network of service providers can address complex needs of families. Often, low-income families and service agencies in these communities do not have the resources or time to access different locations in the community to receive services. Therefore, having an AmeriCorps member accelerate the opening of a community hub is an efficient way to provide a variety of services in one location. The perspectives of people in the community are an important component for bringing forth a diverse, committed network to achieve local Community Partnership goals. Furthermore, AmeriCorps members serve as advocates for families and relay their stories to site supervisors. They increase network diversity and boost site capacity by bring both their own perspective and other community perspectives.

Our Response

- Local Community Partnership host sites continue to provide adequate supports and resources for AmeriCorps member to do outreach and education in communities they serve.

- Use AmeriCorps members to motivate a variety of service providers to do outreach.
- Identify ways/tools for people in the community to learn more about Community Partnerships and potentially recruit people who bring a diversity of perspectives.

SUMMARY

This impact project examined two basic questions: (1) What deep and lasting impacts result from AmeriCorps members' service at Community Partnership sites, and (2) What modifications in the AmeriCorps Partnering to Protect Children program are recommended to facilitate progress toward attaining desired outcomes.

Several insights were reinforced and increased through the project impact evaluation process. Especially important is that AmeriCorps members and their host site supervisors need to have a solid understanding of the following:

- Goals and responsibilities of AmeriCorps members in general and the AmeriCorps Partnering to Protect Children program in particular.
- Philosophy and approach of the Community Partnership to Protect Children state-wide initiative.
- Mentor-mentee relationship of Community Partnership host site supervisors and AmeriCorps members.
- Local context and goals identified by the specific Community Partnership host site at which the AmeriCorps member serves.

The host site supervisor were asked to answer the online survey open-ended question, "What are some of the changes that were noticed related to involvement of AmeriCorps." The six respondents who answered this question reinforced that progress has been made toward achieving desired outcomes of the AmeriCorps Partnering to Protect Children program. They stated:

- "We are able to have a larger presence in the community."
- "More structure, more involvement from [Community Partnership] members, more understanding, excitement."
- "In a few months, the member was able to meet with and talk about [Community Partnership] projects with more community stakeholders that we would have been able to do in years. Particularly effective meeting with and engaging churches and ministerial associations."
- "Visibility of CPPC, understanding of CPPC, links between CPPC and [Domestic Violence]."
- "The service providers and community members are more open to discuss [local Community Partnership] and the gaps/needs. More information is being discussed out in the community.'
- "Increased community awareness and engagement."

For seven of the eight online survey respondents, the number of community organizations the Community Partnership currently engages with average 18.7 (ranged from 3 to 50). The eighth respondent did not report a specific number, but wrote the program is statewide.

RECOMMENDATIONS

Building on the successes of our initial year 2014-2015 program and insights gained through the impact project, the AmeriCorps Partnering to Protect Children program leadership/administrators can make several relatively small changes in programming for 2015-2016 that could impact greater program success. These are:

- Include local host site-specific goals as part of the host site agreement.
- Provide Host Site Supervisors with recruiting and interviewing tips, tools, and assistance in helping host sites find the right member, as opposed to finding someone to fill the position.
- Adapt orientation content and follow-up meetings to review and reinforce the goals of AmeriCorps, AmeriCorps Partnering to Pro-

tect Children, and Community Partnerships to Protect Children.

- Provide a member-orientation checklist for AmeriCorps host site supervisors that includes the member and supervisor developing a plan for ongoing mentorship.
- Facilitate trainings that will help AmeriCorps members achieve the program specific performance measurements and goals laid out in the grant application.
- Work with the Iowa State University (ISU) Community Partnership specialist employed through the contract between ISU and the Iowa Department of Human Services to develop a plan for sharing program tips and tools across partnership sites.
- Include and expand opportunities for AmeriCorps members to develop a deeper awareness of their own specific skillsets and how to apply and develop their skills during their service year.
- Offer and expect attendance at regional meetings for AmeriCorps members and Community Partnership host site supervisors during which resources, tips and tools will be shared among meeting participants.
- Develop an AmeriCorps Partnering to Protect Children newsletter to distribute electronically to members and their host site supervisors.
- Encourage AmeriCorps members and host site supervisors to develop and coordinate interactive tools and to use social media to increase sharing and promotion of Community Partnerships across sites throughout Iowa.
- Expect AmeriCorps members to keep a portfolio throughout their term of service as a way to track and reflect upon their service experience and their progress toward achieving site-specific goals identified in the host site service agreement.

LIMITATIONS

Multiple limitations to this analysis exist, including sample size. The online quantitative survey was answered by eight of the nine interviewees.

The data were collected mid-way during the first year of the AmeriCorps Partnering to Protect Children began. AmeriCorps members had been placed in November 2014 whereas the interview and online survey responses were collected, respectively, in June and July 2015.

CONCLUSIONS

As a result of participating in the Impact Project, the project team leadership with the AmeriCorps Partnering to Protect Children program have gained a deeper appreciation for and understanding of the challenges and opportunities for AmeriCorps members, their host site supervisors, and the local Community Partnerships. Leadership has a deeper commitment to and awareness of ways to support local efforts while respecting and honoring the diversity of local contexts, relationships, needs and goals. Based on this understanding and insight, a number of steps have been taken to help achieve a successful end for the 2014-2015 program year and to lay the groundwork for even greater success during the 2015-2016 program year. As a result of the increased coherence that leadership is bringing to the implementation of our program across its multiple host site, we expect that the program will be empowered to implement activities that support its recently-developed program motto: Partnering to support families and strengthen communities!

INTRODUCTION YOUTH ACHIEVEMENT AMERICORPS PROGRAM, UNITED WAY OF EAST CENTRAL IOWA

Kelli Holubeck, Douglas Griesenauer, Laura Columbus, Darcy Andres, Abby Martin, John Spanczack

Over the course of the 2014 program year (August 2014 – August 2015), Youth Achievement AmeriCorps, through the advisement of Steve Patty at Dialogues in Action, LLC, ran a qualitative analysis of the impact AmeriCorps members have on the children they serve in Cedar Rapids. While quantitative analyses had been performed yearly to measure reading improvement rates and satisfaction surveys had been given to teachers to rate their satisfaction with the program and to give them room for their input, this qualitative analysis allowed Youth Achievement AmeriCorps to dive deeper into the impact AmeriCorps members were having not only on the students' test scores, but on the students themselves.

Program Overview

The Youth Achievement AmeriCorps program, a United Way of East Central Iowa education initiative, leverages the power of national service as well as the strengths of local community partners through the committed service of fifteen full-time AmeriCorps members who provide support to low-income children and families through early literacy programming, literacy tutoring and enrichment, and math tutoring and STEM engagement in an effort to decrease the achievement gap and get kids on track academically and developmentally. Each Youth Achievement AmeriCorps member serves 1700 hours over the course of the year providing service in the Cedar Rapids community enhancing a pipeline of high-quality in and out-of-school time education programs, from birth through middle school to help lessen the achievement gap in the community between lower-income youth and their higher-income peers. As the majority of the AmeriCorps members in Youth Achievement AmeriCorps provide literacy tutoring to elementary-aged children, this analysis focused around the literacy component of the program.

The Youth Achievement AmeriCorps program works to increase the number of low-income students who are proficient in reading by investing significant service in five local elementary schools in Cedar Rapids. Ten Youth Achievement AmeriCorps members assist students in their literacy needs by:

- Providing one-on-one intervention with students targeted to needs identified in district diagnostic assessments.
- Facilitating small group tutoring based on student needs identified in district diagnostics.
- Engaging in holistic support by building relationships with students in enrichment programming.

METHODOLOGY

21 teachers, learning strategists, and AmeriCorps host site supervisors were identified for interviews in the spring of 2015. Due to scheduling conflicts and other complications, 10 interviews were conducted across four of the five schools. Interviews were conducted by trained volunteers and Social Work practicum students in order to ensure objectivity in both the recording of responses and to ensure honest responses from the participants. Interviews lasted approximately 45 minutes and consisted of 20 questions that ranged from surface questions (e.g. How does (the student) feel about reading?) to deeper questions (e.g. How is this program developing a strength of identity as a reader?). The full list can be found in the appendix. Question topics include:

- Student motivation to learn.
- Student increased ability to read.
- Student increased engagement in school.
- Improved at-school behavior of students.
- Increased teacher efficiency/effectiveness as a result of AmeriCorps support.

FINDINGS

Through analysis of each of the ten interviews, seven findings were elucidated from the conversations. While quantitative and qualitative findings do support the belief that Youth Achievement AmeriCorps increases reading rates, what is more surprising is the great impact AmeriCorps members have in building the confidence and sense of efficacy in the students they see.

Finding #1: Confidence as a cornerstone to learning

Description

Nearly every individual interviewed expressed confidence as an impressive result of AmeriCorps intervention. This is interesting because, before the interviews were conducted, the team members assumed that increasing literacy would have been the first thought from most teachers regarding this program, as it is at its core a literacy intervention. While literacy rates do improve because of Youth Achievement AmeriCorps, the first comment from most interviewees was at the amount of confidence that students gained as a result of being paired with an AmeriCorps tutor. Those interviewed mentioned how AmeriCorps members are not just teaching students how to read, but they are teaching students that they have the ability to do something, to keep trying even if something is hard, and to be able to ask for help if they need it. Nearly every interview expressed the change that happened in students throughout the year from one of feeling self-defeated when it came to reading to feeling excited about reading, even if they struggled a little.

This confidence is also reported to extend beyond the intervention time. Teachers and support staff report that this confidence continues on when the student is in other classes and continues with the student throughout the year. Consistently, multiple interviews expressed how the students now believe that "they can do it", which improves their entire demeanor and attitude toward reading and school.

> "The student growth is tremendous. They are able to site down and pay attention longer. They have confidence in their abilities and are not judged (by the AmeriCorps members) if they get it wrong. Their overall classroom behavior has improved. They are no longer asked repeatedly to do things they can't or don't want to do. They now have confidence that they can do it and have greater participation." (Site coordinator)

> "Now in the classroom students volunteer more to read than they did at the beginning of the year. The positive reinforcement of behaviors by the AmeriCorps is huge as the students get rewarded when they do well. This change in behaviors and skills has been seen in the classroom." (1st grade teacher)

> "Students learn to attack lessons head on, persevere and don't give up. After the AmeriCorps support they feel that they can do it." (Learning strategist)

> "Confidence that continued to be evident through and until the end of the school year… These students ask questions in the classroom where they did not before. They exhibit the ability to learn independently. They exhibit determination…completing the activities assigned, and having greater engagement in group work and also in individual work." (Elementary teacher)

Significance

This aspect of confidence is significant because it increases the impact of the AmeriCorps intervention to much more than just increasing reading rates. By understanding that through their consistent interaction with students, AmeriCorps members become defacto mentors for these students, Youth Achievement AmeriCorps interventions can be seen in a much broader context as improving not only reading rates in children who need supports, but also improving social and emotional skills in these students as well.

Our Response

In response to this information, Youth Achievement AmeriCorps can now be much more intentional and directional with our supports around building confidence. This can be done in a variety of ways:

- Trainings can be established specifically around building confidence in order to solidify these skills for all members.

- Specific focus can be made around building intentional self-efficacy in students in order to capitalize on this confidence-building and encourage greater sense of self in students.

- Counselors and supervisors can also be encouraged to share their ideas around social/emotional learning in order to build a culture of confidence in all schools.

- It would be interesting to observe as well if this confidence continues in later years even without AmeriCorps involvement, and interviews may be taken in subsequent years to test this hypothesis.

Finding #2 –Building and rebuilding motivation and trust

Description

Youth Achievement AmeriCorps is designed to target those areas of our community that are most in need of additional supports. As such, it is not surprising to note that those students engaged in this program come from families that are under-resourced and considerably over-burdened. Research fro Adverse Childhood Experiences (ACEs) supports this theory as "Traumatic events make it difficult for children to trust. They make it difficult to feel worthy, take initiative, and form relationships."

Through these interviews, the team discovered that AmeriCorps members are in a unique relationship to help student build, or rebuild, trust with a caring adult. Through being an adult role model that simply, yet genuinely, cares about these students, the AmeriCorps members build trust and motivation in these students.

Especially for these students, reading can be very difficult as knowing they are not the best readers further compromises their motivation. AmeriCorps members combat this by offering consistent positive reinforcement and by creating a virtuous cycle as students learn to read, which increases their motivation and, in turn, further encourages reading.

"The students the AmeriCorps are working with don't come from an environment where trust is easily expressed and felt. Students need to develop this trust with the AmeriCorps to feel supported... Students have learned through AmeriCorps to respect, build trust with an adult, have responsibility, and the importance of saying what you want to do. The respect part is huge." (Learning Strategist)

"AmeriCorps are another adult relationship where students can go to and talk. They are happy to see them and read with them. They also work on their writing skills. The students see the AmeriCorps member every day and are scheduled consistently." (Teacher)

"Students values have changed (because of AmeriCorps) in their ability to try hard, putting forth effort to get where they want and valuing other individual's help. A kid in the beginning of the year was very disengaged and did not want to do any of the work. As he built the relationship with the AmeriCorps member and practiced skills he learned that he can do it and learned the importance of working hard. Students seek out other opportunities for learning and growth when they share with another individual of their skills and learn when they build relations with a school person who cares and building trust with a caring adult." (Learning Strategist)

"AmeriCorps (as well as teachers) create that stable positive support in student's lives. This is important as students are used to not getting that support at home. AmeriCorps are able to be that positive adult role model for students at (the school)." (Teacher)

Significance

This building of trust and motivation is key as it allows students to build lasting skills that, again, reach far beyond literacy. Once students learn to trust the AmeriCorps members who work with them, they are able to open up in ways that allow deep learning to take place.

Our Response

Knowing this, Youth Achievement AmeriCorps can work toward learning how to jumpstart this motivation. Learning skills such as Motivational Interviewing may allow AmeriCorps members to build rapport with their students even fast, thus catalyzing the trust necessary to spur motivation. Of course, any trust takes time, and so these tools must be buffered with the insistence that trust and motivation be created through genuine relationships with these students. This organic relationship that occurs through a mentoring relationship must be carefully cultivated in order to reach the greatest impact.

Finding #3 – Teamwork: creating colleagues in learning

Description

School staff are deeply grateful for AmeriCorps members assisting those in need, though a student's education does not ever rely solely on one program or person. As such, those interviewed noted how the relationship between Youth Achievement AmeriCorps, the schools, and other programming is key in order to ensure that those students most in need are successful. They noted how the combination of classroom instruction and AmeriCorps investment allowed students to build connections throughout the class day. They also noted that because of the specific role of AmeriCorps members serving "bubble kids" or those who need some additional supports, but who are not in need of trained teacher interventions, teachers are able to concentrate more fully on students who are in greater need for attention.

> "The strategies that are taught in PREP are the same in the classroom. This allows kids to stay connected and gives them a consistent approach in solving problems." (Learning Strategist)

> "The AmeriCorps add to this love that I try to create as the students know they have another someone who is there and cares about them." (Teacher)

> "Teachers enjoy (the AmeriCorps members). Because of the AmeriCorps members, teachers have the time to work with other kids. They feel it is a blessing and nice to have them there. The teachers can focus on the kids that are further behind and the AmeriCorps members can focus on the kids that are lacking some skills." (Host Site Supervisor)

Significance

Relationships are key to any successful program, and knowing that the connections and relationships are being built in schools is essential. That being said, it is also significant to note that this response was not noted in all schools that were interviewed. Therefore, while success is seen in some schools, more could be done in order to cement the relationship between the AmeriCorps program and the schools that are being served.

Our Response

In response to this, Youth Achievement AmeriCorps can take the best practices from those schools who do build successful relationships with members and encourage all other schools to replicate these successes. By engaging members in the schools, both structurally in meetings and physically in where they are located in the building, schools can develop a richer experience with their members. Also, even successful schools can be encouraged to document their best practices and brainstorm how they can further engage their members in their work.

Finding #4: Embracing your intelligence: Reading vs Being a reader

Description

Of course, the academic improvement was still noted as being a tremendous asset of the program. AmeriCorps support with these students allows them to take ownership as readers. This expands their view of themselves and what they can do. As such, they find more opportunities to read and are more likely to want to be called on in class in order to display their skills.

What is interesting to note, though, is that in addition to reading skills, those interviewed also mentioned how students are now also showing engagement in their learning. They are increasing their identities as readers which expands how they think of the world around them. As a result of reading interventions, students now ask questions and apply their readings to other contexts or situations. This critical thinking goes far beyond reading, as it is the beginning of them making sense of the world around them and demanding that their voice be heard.

"An AmeriCorps recently pulled a child from class who was struggling to meet the 60 words per minute goal. He was reading about 6 words per minute and in the six weeks he has worked with the AmeriCorps has increased his fluency score to 22 words per minute." (Teacher)

"From the AmeriCorps evaluation, students are better readers. They have seen growth in students in PREP 1 (the reading intervention). Students look at learning differently. It is no longer as much of a chore as when they started. Students want to be there as they have built a relationship with the AmeriCorps." (Learning Strategist)

"Students show Interest in the subject matter and engagement in learning ... They show self-motivation in that they will pick up a book without external motivation ... The program supported the student in 'seeing' themselves as a reader." (Teacher)

"[The AmeriCorps] modelled in the beginning, and now it is

more of a collaborative approach. The students are making connections and integrating words into their everyday life. (For example, when talking about play, students recognized when they play and what that looks like.)" (Learning Strategist)

"At the beginning of the school year these students do not care about education and by the end of the school year they care about learning. This curiosity and care about learning expands to other subject areas." (Teacher)

Significance

This change from simply increasing reading scores, as the quantitative analysis proves Youth Achievement AmeriCorps does, to creating students who identify as readers is big. While improving scores is a very positive result of the program, creating individuals who self-select as readers expands the programs efficacy well-beyond the doors of the classroom. Readers are more likely to display their skills and read independently. This internal change in a student allows the effect of the intervention to last well-beyond the tone of the school bell.

Our Response

In response to this, Youth Achievement AmeriCorps can continue to be more deliberate in its actions in creating readers instead of just students who can read. Some ways to encourage this transformation to occur includes:

- Helping students feel valued and building their self-efficacy when they read.
- Celebrating their efforts instead of their effects so that they internalize their work.
- Making connections to what students enjoy so that reading can be a way to expand their own preferences and hobbies.
- Being proud of the student as a reader and reinforcing this concept with teachers, parents, and other adults in the students' lives.

Finding #5: A safe place creates a calm mind

Description

Sometimes students who experience stressful situations just need a place where they can feel safe and deescalate from what is going on. By providing 1 on 1 or small group interventions with a caring mentor in a safe location, the AmeriCorps members are able to provide this calming environment. More than one school reported that they have seen students who normally have behavior problems are now solving their problems and practicing conflict resolution as a result of AmeriCorps intervention.

Those interviewed also noted that in conjunction with having a safe space, improving reading skills also reduced disruptive behavior. Some teachers reported that students may act up because they feel scared when they can't read and are called upon to do so in class. By engaging in avoidance behaviors and trying to appeal to the teacher, they disrupt the classroom environment. The teachers have seen this behavior be reduced through AmeriCorps literacy interaction, and believe the combination of the reading skills and being cared for make this happen.

> "The office is a calm place out of class where students can better focus and engage in their learning. For example, one student was having motivational and focus issues in the afternoon but with AmeriCorps intervention moved to the morning, they were able to make it through the entire day." (Host site supervisor)

> "AmeriCorps know student's home life and issues with peers in the classroom. They can follow-up with teacher s and parents. This shows students that they care and value them. Students in the elementary level are the 'beginning of their journey.' They need staff who care about them academically and cater to their socio-emotional needs." (Host site supervisor)

> "At the start of the year, the students were very shy and didn't speak a lot. Now they are not in the office everyday, doing better in class, more likely to sit down and pay attention when

told. They have bigger friend groups and approach different adults even in the halls. Overall, they are more open." (Host site supervisor)

Significance

No student, or any adult, can cleanly separate their academic lives from their personal lives. As such, schools must strike a delicate balance between ensuring that academic benchmarks are reached while acknowledging the trauma that many children face, especially those in neighborhood with fewer resources. AmeriCorps members have the opportunity to provide this safety and balance due to the 1 on 1 or small group nature of their relationship.

Our Response

Much like many of the above responses, paying greater attention to the structure and training of Youth Achievement AmeriCorps program in light of these responses is key to building an effective response. Some ideas for ensuring that this safety is ubiquitous includes:

- Having a plan for AmeriCorps members to follow in case a student cannot self-regulate his or her behaviors.
- Asking the students for feedback if they are having trouble calming themselves. This may include asking students where they feel safest when they are not in crisis.
- Ensuring that members know who to contact if the student is in need of more professional services.

Another interesting response would be to compare behavioral data from those engaged in the program against those who have not in order to confirm the qualitative information received. This quantitative support would allow us to further target areas that we can celebrate success and target new interventions.

Finding #6: Multiplying impact – adding in volunteerism

Description

While the information we found in these interviews is eye-opening, what can be equally important is what was not said in the interviews. A topic that all interviewed omitted was the impact that members have on volunteerism in their schools. While AmeriCorps members do engage their schools in recruiting and managing volunteers, as volunteerism is a core tenant of AmeriCorps, none of those interviewed discussed these responsibilities that took place.

Significance

This is significant as there seems to be a disconnection between the volunteer recruitment and management taking place by the members and the impact that this work has in multiplying the impact at the schools. As the questions were specifically around the students, those interviewed did not seem to make that connection on their own that the volunteer recruitment being done also impacts the outcomes of the students. Either that or those interviewed were either not aware that the volunteer recruitment was being done by the members or were not aware of the recruitment at all.

Our Response

In response to this, an emphasis on the volunteer work in communication with the sites is essential as well as ensuring that this message is passed down to the teachers who interact with the members and students. By sharing this information with the schools, all staff at the schools, from Learning Supports to host site supervisors to teachers, can be more aware of the impact that National Service is having on these schools.

Finding #7: Everyone wins: benefits to students, teachers AND members

Description

The final finding from these interviews is not about the students at all. After review common themes from all interviews, it should be noted that Youth Achievement AmeriCorps does not only impact the students it explicitly serves, but it also impacts the teachers involved as well as the AmeriCorps members themselves. The teachers report not being able to reach as many children as they are without AmeriCorps support and also report that they know the children would not be where they are now without AmeriCorps members. They also report that AmeriCorps members grow from the support they give to each other. As they progress through the year, staff see members' skills maturing as they are able to discuss deeper issues and can share skills with each other that allow them to be more effective in their work. The teachers report how members now gain ownership of their skills and can truly make a strong impact in the children they serve.

"I couldn't say enough about the support AmeriCorps provided." (Learning Strategist)

"A teacher this morning interacted with an AmeriCorps wanting the number for a parent and how to best say their child was having issues. Teachers have given glowing remarks about the skills and growth of both of the members. AmeriCorps members brainstorm and practice trial and error situations with teachers and develop a targeted plan for intervention." (Savino)

"I feel blessed because of the support I have received in my first year of teaching. I feel very lucky to have received that support and know much of the progress I have seen this year is a result of the time the AmeriCorps have spent with the children in my classroom. I am also very grateful for the AmeriCorps support and could not have done it without them." (1st grade teacher)

Significance

Oftentimes the impact that this program has on others is overlooked for the targeted success seen in the students. While of course student improvement is fundamental to the program's success, it should also be noted that this program's impact goes far beyond student achievement. Youth Achievement AmeriCorps allows teachers to continue to give their best work in the schools and also deeply builds the skills and abilities of the members who serve. These skills should not be ignored as we evaluate the success of this program on its community.

Our Response

In response to this, we need to make sure that we take time to celebrate our achievements. Our Program Manager has been doing amazing work already in making this happen by celebrating the successes of our members both for those new who comes at the beginning of the year and especially for those who are leaving. Youth Achievement AmeriCorps will continue to celebrate these successes and pay special attention to the growth and development that happens to all who engage in this rewarding work.

CONCLUSION

In conclusion, while the efficacy of the reading intervention was established and strong before this evaluation, these qualitative interviews have given the members of Youth Achievement AmeriCorps a much deeper understanding of the real impact of our program outside of the narrow lens of literacy. This new information, coupled with our commitment to continuously improve our literacy programming, will allow Youth Achievement AmeriCorps to provide the greatest benefit to those students entrusted to us.

Other quotations of note that did not fit cleanly into the above findings include:

"Students' future Is dependent on a well developed sense of control over their destiny. AmeriCorps can help kids develop this sense of control with strategies for solving problems when they are reading or else where. The AmeriCorps program helps develop those skills for success." (Learning strategist)

"(The AmeriCorps) was a positive role model for the students. The student was able to see a positive role model as opposed to just "hearing" what positive behavior was." (Teacher)

"AmeriCorps members are student's cheerleaders." (Learning strategist)

Next steps will involve qualitative measurement of the students themselves. This first round of evaluations consisted of educators who interacted with students in order to gain a deeper understanding of those who were familiar with the organizational structure of the program. We would like to refine these questions to target the elementary students themselves to see if they perceive the same change in their own behaviors. There will be some complications with adjusting the questionnaire to appeal to a younger audience, but we believe that this information will be valuable as we continue to improve our program.

AmeriCorps 4-H Outreach Program, Iowa State University—Extension and Outreach, 4-H Youth Development

Susan Hollenkamp

INTRODUCTION

From February-August 2015, the Iowa AmeriCorps 4-H Outreach Project Impact team worked together to develop a new strategy for measuring AmeriCorps program youth participant experiences. This process has given our team, for the first time ever, a guide for conducting evaluation of AmeriCorps program youth participant experiences through qualitative data research and analysis. Prior to our participation in the Seeing Impact Project, Iowa AmeriCorps 4-H Outreach conducted program youth participant surveys to evaluate program impact. The first survey was conducted prior to the start of the program, and the final survey was conducted at the conclusion of the program. The survey measured the program youth participant's progress by using a multiple choice and 'yes' or 'no' method to evaluate program impact. Participation in the Seeing Impact Project has encouraged our team to develop a more thoughtful way for our program staff to measure program impact on the AmeriCorps programming participants. This report presents our findings that are based on a series of interviews designed to delve deeper into the impact our program has had on its youth participants. Furthermore this report offers a plan of action to be implemented by program staff to assist them in accomplishing the impact of AmeriCorps programming on Iowa AmeriCorps 4-H Outreach program youth participants.

METHODOLOGY

For the purpose of the Seeing Impact Project, we conducted in-person interviews with 65 Iowa AmeriCorps 4-H Outreach program participants located in both rural and urban communities. Of the 65 participants who were interviewed all were high school students. Each interview lasted approximately 45 minutes and was facilitated by each of our team members. The interview questions focused on the following topics:

- Civic Engagement -- Continuing to be engaged in service to one's community upon completion of program.

- Future Aspirations -- How the program has influenced the future goals and aspirations of the youth participant.

- Problem Solving -- How the youth participant overcame a conflict or particularly difficult situation.

- Overcoming Fear -- How the youth participant overcame a fear of being his or her's own true self, public speaking, doing something they've never do before.

- Developing Self-Confidence -- How the youth participant developed self-confidence throughout the course of the program, and what the youth participant feels they could do now, that they thought they couldn't do before participating in the program.

Finding 1: Leadership

Description

A common theme that presented itself during the interview process was the development of leadership ability among the students involved in the program. Highlights of this theme included a turning point in the program during which the students discovered their ability to lead. These turning points ranged from experiencing a successful service project to partnering with a legislator.

Service project success

"I was nervous at first, but afterward I learned that if you have a passion for it, you can do it!"

"Service is a necessity; a leader leads by serving and leads by example."

"I am more confident now trying out for leadership positions in the future."

"Being a leader means keeping your word and staying committed to a project until it is completed."

Public speaking event

"At first, it was hard and I didn't know what to expect. It was successful, and I feel like I will be able to successfully give another presentation in the future. I've grown as a person and as a professional."

Significance

This finding highlighted the positive impact different AmeriCorps programs have on the individual growth of each student involved in the program. The core of this finding is the transformation that occurs when students experience the "Ah, ha!" moment and realize they are leaders. This finding also shows that when students are offered opportunities to lead, and are encouraged to do so and feel supported by their mentors, the students will succeed and will gain the confidence in themselves to participate in other leadership roles in the future.

Our Response:

- Discover more ways students can hold leadership positions within their communities. This would include being a youth representative on a board.
- Continue to implement training for staff and students on the different styles of leadership
- Encourage involvement among students and emphasize the importance of holding leadership roles.

Finding 2: Future Aspirations

Description

A common theme that presented itself during the interview process was recognition of future career goals. A few of our programs have students between the ages of 15-18. This is typically the age when students begin to think about what they want to do after they graduate high school. Do they want to go onto college? Do they want to join the workforce right away? Do they want to join the military or other national service organization? These are the kinds of questions that were discussed during the interview process. Highlights of this finding were responses indicating where the students see themselves after they graduate high school and where they see themselves in 5 years, specifically after being involved in the program.

> "I've learned the importance of serving others and about how to address issues; I've become very passionate about service and doing things for others. I have a newfound interest in having a career in law and/or service."

> "I'd like to start my own NGO or work for one after college. I am interested in the global health track for a career. This program has inspired me to help people in some sort of way."

> "I'd like to attend Georgetown University and study political science. This program [SIYAC] is the best thing. It has helped me find my voice and is encouraging me to reach my full potential."

> "I was never interested or involved in service learning or advocacy prior to SIYAC. Now I want to keep doing it."

Significance

This finding highlights the ways in which AmeriCorps programming positively impacts the future of our youth members. Giving students the opportunities to hold leadership roles when they're younger makes it more likely for them to try out for leadership roles in the future; it has "conditioned" them for using what they learn in the AmeriCorps program and contributing it to their future. In addition, after being involved in the program's mission to address community issues through service learning, students change their future goals and aspirations to include opportunities for service learning.

This finding implies that AmeriCorps programs are not only providing opportunities for students to become leaders and achieve their goals in the present, AmeriCorps programs continue to provide opportunities for students to become leaders and achieve their goals well into the future.

Our Response:
- Discover more opportunities for youth to get involved in mentorship programs.
- Foster conversation between staff and students regarding future aspirations and maintaining a life well-lived (and defining what that means for students).
- Develop ways for youth to map their goals and steps to achieve said goals.

Finding 3: Volunteerism

Description

A common theme that presented itself during the interview process was the development of an appreciation for serving one's community. The participants we interviewed described how facilitating a service project is important in their role as a citizen of a community. There was an interesting range of responses from interviewees regarding the challenges faced while initiating a service project. Some students were able to plan projects with no problem, while others experienced difficulties in almost every aspect including research, planning, community support, and volunteer recruitment. These challenges at times would negatively affect the student's determination, however, with positive reinforcement from members, our findings show that service project facilitation and volunteerism can also lead towards growth in other aspects of their lives, including leadership ability, confidence in own voice, and awareness of issues affecting their communities.

Leadership Ability/Confidence

"I have really matured in that [public speaking] aspect and becoming a leader on the Council has helped me to do so. It has been very beneficial in getting over my fears of saying something wrong or being a youth and talking to an adult; I'm not afraid to take charge or lead a project anymore."

Awareness of issues affecting their communities

"While researching service projects and issues in my community, I found that there are more issues in my community than I had realized. By addressing those issues through service, I was able to create a positive change in my community."

Significance

This finding highlighted the successes AmeriCorps programs have in regards to providing youths the opportunities to engage in service learning projects. Since we have the mission of providing positive youth development, we find it important to our program that members fully understand the impact of volunteerism and service learning for communities so that we can continue to offer students the opportunities to serve and grow as community leaders. This finding also highlights the different aspects in which youth can grow professionally and personally; service project facilitation, coordination and participation fosters confidence, determination and the importance of staying connected to one's community.

Our Response:

- Continue to emphasize with site staff and members the importance of service learning and facilitating service projects with the students.
- Foster more opportunities for youth-planned activities
- Develop new ways to identify community needs

Finding 4: Self Confidence "Success Breeds Confidence"

Youth in the program talked repeatedly about struggling with low self-esteem. This often contributed to youth struggling with depression, anxiety, and social disengagement. Ensuring the program offered frequent and varied opportunities for self-expression provided youth a way to not only safely express feelings but to experience accomplishment and success. In turn, artistic expression led to positive feedback for their accomplishments from peers, staff and the community. One example would be youth artists learning an advanced art skill in a program workshop, preparing the art in a gallery show, and hosting the community gallery show.

> "The bass playing got me out (of home) more and talking to people, I started playing more and it's something I thought I'd never do."

> "It's showed me that I'm capable of doing a lot more and I should do a lot more."

> "I was never really was able to express myself through my art. Now, you can see the emotion in the colors I use."

> "I've been very involved in the arts part of the program. It helped me find myself and my identity."

> "Being in a place with other musicians it gave me an opportunity to like talk to them and a conversation blooms out of that." I feel like it's (the program) has brought me closer to the community."

One young person talked about how she gave her first presentation at a nonprofit event with dozens of people in attendance. She was nervous, and experienced anxiety and self-doubt when developing and creating her presentation. However, the presentation turned out to be a success, and she identified an increase in her public speaking skills as a result of participating in the presentation. She said she is confident that she will be able to successfully give another presentation in the future. Her words were, "I've just grown as a person and as a professional."

Another youth filled a vacant filled a vacant leadership position on the Council, she was nervous about how well she would do in the position because she didn't feel like she had enough experience to be successful. However, with encouragement from her peers and coordinator, she stuck with the position. And the Council's success in facilitating and completing service projects improved ten-fold. She told us, "I am more confident now trying out for leadership positions in the future."

Significance

The finding highlighted the importance of providing a variety of opportunities for youth to express themselves. Not all youth find success through traditional avenues and providing an area of opportunities for youth to learn new skills and see growth in self-esteem. Youth often feel more comfortable expresses their feelings through the arts. This offers them a safe way to express their thoughts as well as to achieve mastery of a skill.

Our Response

- Staff at programs will develop activities that utilize artistic self-expression into the group activities.
- Staff will work seek volunteers to teach arts activities to youth group. Volunteers will provide expertise in visual art, music, dance, drama or any art form that encourages learning, self-expression and success.
- Youth will help staff define what arts activities they have interest in and ways to show the community what they have learned and created through art shows, recordings and the like.

Finding 5: Social Anxiety/Acceptance "Free To Be Me"

Youth in the program consistently identified feeling socially anxious when joining groups and in new social situations. This finding was not surprising but the nearly universal noting of it was. Nearly every youth found the acceptance in the group as a key to feeling relaxed and enjoying the group. Interviews showed that positive staff/youth rapport was key to helping youth feel comfortable in the beginning. Ensuring that group activities provide opportunities for participants to get to know each other and have fun also helped youth feel accepted, befriended and comfortable. In addition, youth talked about the safe opportunity to practice and successfully speak in front of the group as a specific area of improvement.

"I don't have very good social skills but they've gotten better".

"I'm better at talking to people and more confident"

"The biggest thing was I couldn't talk to people (before attending the program), it was nerve wracking just to try and talk to somebody."

"I used to think I was doing something wrong [when interacting with peers]. Getting past that has made me feel better about myself"

"I had chance to meet a lot of people that I wouldn't have met and have learned lots of ways to exercise better and eat better".

"I'm not as shy now. It used to take me hours to go and talk to somebody. Even to ask where the restroom is was scary to me."

"I've been a lot more social. I made friends here, I go to school and see them, and I've made friends with their friends."

"It's actually made it easier for me to go up and talk to teachers because the adults here are easy going and put a positive outlook on adults and I see them as safer now."

"I have anxiety issue, particularly in social situations, and being here helped that. When I first started going here about like three years ago I didn't really talk much I just sort of just stood around, but now I'm a lot more active with people."

"The hardest thing I had to learn to do was actually being able to approach new people. When I first came here I had to force myself to approach new people. I felt like a fish in a new sea. It's made me better at joining in on a conversation and not make it awkward".

"A few times I've been asked to go up and speak in front of a few people." "Even though my social anxiety is much less now (as a result of the program) to this day I fear public speaking." (Still, he acknowledges that he was able to do it and is proud he went through with it. It's showed him "what will happen will happen" and to try not to panic.)

"I've had a lot of positive experiences here. I'm slowly starting to make new friends, slowly starting to be able to socialize with people, and being able to find other people to share common interests."

"I felt it intimidating to express own opinion on certain youth issues." [But after working with her peers on service projects and position statements, I realize] "the other members were always supportive , and so it helped me to stand up and share my own opinions."

"I became a leader for youth and have gained confidence to address issues facing Iowa's youth and to use my voice." (She has become more talkative and confident in her voice as a result of participating in youth discussions and service projects. Prior to SIYAC, she was a timid student and was hesitant to speak up for fear of being wrong.)

Significance

The finding highlighted the all too common experience of feeling unaccepted, misunderstood, and not part of the group. It showed the need for additional and more varied community opportunities for youth who feel disenfranchised to feel welcomed and accepted. In addition it showed the need for youth development professionals to be aware of group dynamics and how to consistently have varied levels of opportunities for youth to talk and participate.

Our Response

- Staff at programs will be trained in the Youth Program Quality Assessment protocol for ensuring safe and accepting spaces.
- Staff will provide youth opportunities to practice leadership in groups including youth lead activities and individual time to share thoughts with the group.
- Staff will process in team meetings on an ongoing basis how the group experience can be more welcoming to all and solicit feedback from youth participants.

Finding 6 - Safe Environment "We Belong Here"

This finding is about how the 4H program has helped youth experience a feeling of unconditional respect for who they are and a sense of belonging. Youth experienced ownership of the program. This feature was critical for them to have a sense of shared community. This was accomplished through opportunities to give back through volunteer initiatives, contribute to group activity ideas, and most importantly to have a simple rule of Unconditional Positive Regard (UPR). UPR was explained to all participants during their tour of the facility and youth/staff role model it for each other. This goal of respect for all was woven into all activities and continually reinforced that youth were a key part of ensuring a safe environment for all.

This theme was especially apparent in situations where young people experienced personal challenges during the program. One participant's family, for instance, became homeless during the program. He "talked to people and it became like a home to him." He reflected on how the program helped him with "having things to do. It kept my mind off of it." A student went through the difficult time of losing her grandmother during the first month of her service on SIYAC. She said the experience was "hard not only for personal reasons, but I also felt like I was letting the Council down. But everyone on the council was very supportive during that time."

The sense of belonging forged during the program impacted the youth in many ways. The following are examples of how the youth talked about this finding:

"People were nicer than kids in my school and I realized this was a place I could actually talk to people and not be afraid."

"I wasn't used to going out and I didn't like to talk to people. I was too shy. But since coming to the program, I'm getting used to it. Now, if I need help I'll ask for it."

"Originally I wanted to join the workout group but I was nervous about it because everyone knew each other. But I decided to do because (staff) encouraged me."

"[The group participants] helped me feel comfortable expressing my opinions and thoughts. It helped me feel comfortable being who I am and ok being into things that are considered weird or nerdy".

"I'm involved in a couple of clubs in my school and we started using UPR as reminder to keep things positive and build each other up rather than knock each other down."

"I felt very connected to SIYAC and everyone on the Council; we were close and just great friends despite differing opinions. Other students sparked my interest in new things such as science and philosophy. I enjoyed the program because the students challenged one another, and with that, they helped each other grow."

Significance

The finding highlighted that it is possible through trained and attentive staff to have programming and groups that follow one simple rule of respect for each other. Teaching this simple concept through coaching and practice shows youth that "treating others how you'd like to be treated" is possible throughout one's life and results in positive based problem solving and relationships.

Our Response

- Staff at programs will be trained in the concept of Unconditional Positive Regard (respect for all).

- Individual programs will adopt this policy of respect for all to help ensure participants feel welcomed, safe, and accepted.

- Youth program participants will brainstorm in groups what feeling respected looks like, feels like and sounds like.

Finding 7: Community

A common theme that presented itself during the interview process was 'community.' By 'community' we mean the experience of young people being a part of something positive that breeds youth involvement, community service, and the feeling of belonging to the greater community. An important aspect of the program that youth pointed out during interviews is that by participating in a team-centered environment with the shared mission of accomplishing a common goal, the youth felt that they were contributing to something bigger than themselves, and therefore felt like they belonged to the program and the community. Through this feeling of belonging to something bigger than themselves, youth were able to confidently develop their voices and become involved in their community. In addition, a majority of youth drew connections between their peers in the program and a family; they felt safe, supported, and respected.

"The other members inspired me; it was rewarding to be inspired by their work ethic, commitment to service and youth issues."

"[There is now a] willingness to call one another and email one another, and the commitment each of the members had to accomplish their set goals, is what kept [her] going."

"It felt awesome to advocate as team to combat bullying in schools. It showed me how powerful a small group of mindful youth can be."

"I felt very connected to SIYAC and everyone on the Council; we were close and just great friends despite differing opinions."

Significance

This finding shows that by implementing the notion of youth-centered involvement and teamwork at a young age, youth will be able to develop the confidence needed to successfully become engaged citizens later on in life. Feeling a sense of belonging, especially at a young age when a youth's mental capacity can be vulnerable, is important as it gives youth self-worth and shows them how much their contribution means to a community and to a team.

Our response

- Staff will be trained in conducting team-building retreats for the youth members of the program
- Youth will be given opportunities to lead team-building activities and service projects
- All programs will continue to encourage youth participation and youth involvement in communities.

GREEN IOWA AMERICORPS, UNIVERSITY OF NORTHERN IOWA— CENTER FOR ENERGY AND ENVIRONMENTAL EDUCATION

Ashley Craft, Daniel Luepke-Site Supervisor, Bradley James, Rosie Manzo, Zachary Kotz

INTRODUCTION

From February through August of 2015 the Green Iowa AmeriCorps SIP Evaluation team worked to develop a new and insightful way to learn the impacts of member service experience through a qualitative evaluation. The evaluation aimed to learn how current members and alumni of Green Iowa AmeriCorps feel they were impacted by their service experience. The process of creating the evaluation was not only an eye opening and transformative experience for the evaluation team, but the results led to many new and previously unknown findings regarding the members' experience.

This report presents our findings and recommendations based on a series of thorough interviews conducted with current and former Green Iowa AmeriCorps members in regards to their service experience with the program.

Our question of inquiry is the following:

What impact does the service experience with Green Iowa AmeriCorps have on Members?

Leading up to the start of this extensive evaluation, member service experience had only been evaluated through basic qualitative surveys and informal testimonials. The program was interested in digging deeper to generate a better understanding of what components of a member's service experience had a lasting and significant impact.

Eighteen-question interviews were conducted with current and program alumni dating back three years with the goal of understanding how participation in Green Iowa impacted members' ability to gain future employment, vocational clarity, views on civic engagement, and development of their own abilities. The goal of the questions was to find a way to get beyond the surface level impacts and dig deep enough to see how members have not only been impacted by their service but, in many ways, transformed.

METHODOLOGY

To determine the sample from the interviews, two target populations were identified: current Green Iowa AmeriCorps members and program alumni who exited the program successfully in the past three years. The program did not take the geographical location of the service site or the gender of the member into consideration for the purposes of this evaluation.

Two similar but distinct set of interview questions were created for each population. Each interview lasted between 25 and 45 minutes. All current members were interviewed in person by program staff and evaluation team members, Ashley Craft and Daniel Luepke. All program alumni were interviewed via phone by all members of the evaluation team.

The interviewer was responsible for transcribing and summarizing the key findings from each member or alumni interviewed. Upon completion of the interviews, each group member individually analyzed their findings. Following their analysis, team members met to share findings and discuss emergent themes. Finally, team members met for to identify themes, establish findings, and discuss implications and recommendations.

Creating sections for the final report, more specifically the findings, was delegated to member of the evaluation team. The final report compiled all of the findings for review.

Findings

Below are the seven findings that were established as a result of the qualitative evaluation process. Each finding includes a description of the findings, its significance in relation to member experience, and proposed program response based on the findings.

Finding #1 - Involuntary Impacts of Program Design

Description

One of the most interesting and overwhelming findings from the evaluation is the impact of the program and its requirements on transforming many facets of the personal and professional development of the member. The basic premise of this finding is that a member's feelings, actions, and thoughts are formed by following the requirements of the service experience. These features of behavioral change and identity formation became habit through the experience. It has been said, "You are what you repeatedly do." In every area of our program, members are required to learn, educate, and implement different things. We saw overwhelming evidence through the interviews that current members and alumni are being shaped in their very identity by what they were required to do through their service. And for many, this happened without them even realizing it.

Significance

This finding is quite arguably the most significant of all the findings emerging from this evaluation. By including a variety of requirements through our program design and leadership roles, including a variety of skill-building experiences, civic engagement sessions, professional development opportunities, and challenging work scenarios, the members, at the end of the day, are transformed by what they do.

Because they are given sensitivity training and work with people in need, they develop empathy. By requiring them to push their own boundaries and have large amounts of responsibility, they become more confident, resilient and dependable. Those are not just things they do for a temporary moment. We found through these interviews that it becomes part of their makeup. It becomes who they are. If our program was designed differently – without leadership roles or less variety in service work – this significant impact could be lost.

Proposed Program Response

- Intentional Program Design: By giving thorough and intentional planning to our program desire we are able to ensure that we continue to have these long term and impactful results for our members.

- Stressing importance of program components: Because we have seen how successfully this approach impacts members, it must be presented to incoming members with the same importance.

- Reflection in Monthly Reporting: By having members reflect on requirements that have become new habits for them they can see the transformative impact their daily service experience is having throughout and strive for continued growth.

Finding #2 - The Heart of the Matter: Discovering Purpose through Public Service Experience

Description

The reasons for devoting a year to public service vary greatly among individuals. Through our compilation of alumni interviews, we uncovered reoccurring themes of service motivators and of the sense of purpose gained from serving a term in Green Iowa AmeriCorps. Participants exhibited both intrinsic and extrinsic motivations to join our AmeriCorps program. They were motivated by the desire for practical work experience in the energy conservation field, for the benefits an AmeriCorps member receives, or even for something fun and interesting to do while trying to figure out their next step in life. One participant said, "Green Iowa was a great opportunity and a fun adventure while I found another place to work."

We found that these types of motivational factors relate to

members' personality traits, which we realize are a variable, to some extent, that is out of our control. Another related variable, one which lies more within our control as a program, is the opportunity to help individuals discover their purpose. Response patterns throughout the data portrayed that many members gained a sense of direction and purpose in their lives, even if that was not a key factor in why they chose to serve.

Significance

An individual's motivation and purpose for engaging in public service can largely determine the experience they have, as well as the effort and work put into their service. It is important that individuals desire to leave the program better than when they started, and to have added to, or continued to build on the program's mission and goals. In the same sense, it is also crucial to the member, that they are gaining confidence in their purpose while also making positive contributions to the program. One participant said, "My time in Green Iowa has given me a feeling that I have a purpose, almost an obligation, to do my part to improve the lives of the people in my community."

Proposed Program Response

- Professional Development Planning: At the beginning of the service term year each member will create a professional development plan, outlining desired professional development goals they hope to achieve as part of their service experience.

- Pre & Post Service Assessments: Upon entering and exiting the program, members will complete service motivation assessments to determine any changes in sentiment towards service.

- Monthly Report Adjustments: Through the addition of questions regarding personal professional development to the monthly report document members will have an opportunity to reflect on their purpose at the end of each month. The goals outlined can relate back to future service projects and how accomplishing those projects may reinforce a member's sense of purpose.

- Professional Development Project: Each member will be required to complete a professional development project as part of their service experience. This will require members to actively pursue professional development as part of their service experience that is personal the goals outlined in their professional development plan.

- Alumni Meet-ups: Alumni of the program can be an important resource for current members. By inviting alumni to return to the program for meet and greet type events or to participate in a pen pal program, members will be given a chance to ask questions about why they served and how the program has influenced their lives.

Finding #3 – "Confidence" is Key

Description

One clear theme from the interview data is about the development of personal confidence. Alumni and current members alike spoke about developing a long-term, transferable confidence that was developed as a result of the program. Alumni described a sense of independence and confidence to pursue dreams they may have shied away from previously. One said, "When you feel confident, you exude positivity." In part, confidence developed through an increase in knowledge around a variety of program related subjects. The majority of confidence appeared to stem from experiences that pushed members outside of their comfort zone through basic program service requirements—giving presentations, one on one consultation with homeowners, conducting education events, etc.—and subsequently experiencing personal confidence growth.

Significance

The development of self-confidence through basic program service experience not only allows members to be more effective in every aspect of their service, but it also provides members with a valuable life-skill that will be applicable in any future endeavor, both personal and professional.

This finding is also significant to emphasize that the confidence was built through many new and at times daunting experiences. The variety of the program services helps ensure that members will be tested in a variety of ways that will be challenging and ultimately confidence building. The emphasis on professional development and enrolling members that may have little to no experience in a nonprofit or energy related field is also crucial in providing opportunity for growth, NOT maintenance. If Green Iowa AmeriCorps only enrolled individuals with extensive experience in the program service work, a prediction can be made that the confidence and professional development reported would not be as significant.

Proposed Program Response
- Higher emphasis on self-confidence as a program goal: Prior to this evaluation, developing confidence was not on the radar in terms of a significant member benefit to program staff or members alike. By acknowledging the important role that member confidence plays in service, and member experience, the program can be intentional in targeting training to spur the growth of personal confidence and altering reporting to track changes in confidence and identify potential gaps in confidence (i.e. things that different members don't feel comfortable with).

- Increased Support for Members: If it is understood by members that the program considers their development and increased self-confidence as priority through skill building and overcoming challenges, members will feel more supported through those challenges. By understanding that failure is an anticipated outcome on the path to self-improvement members will have a confident approach to new tasks.

- Confidence-building Requirements: Many alumni reported having to fill requirements as the biggest source of confidence building for them because they were "forced" to step up to the challenge and do things that maybe they hadn't done before. By targeting requirements to provide members with the opportunity to face more challenges (hand-in-hand with increased support for members) hopefully this will provide more opportunities to grow confidence in their abilities.

Finding #4 –Building the Better Me

Description

Self-improvement is an emerging theme for both current members and alumni during our evaluation findings. Self-improvement is not only related to what a member took away from program participation but also how he or she saw the service term as well. As with most things, the desire of the individual had a direct impact on the result and experience. Members who saw their service experience as an opportunity grow, learn, and embrace self-improvement were able to squeeze every last drop out of their time with the program. During the interviews, they were able to share in great detail how the program provided them with the opportunity for self-improvement. Those who had little desire of using their service term to improve themselves did not identify the same type of impact, though the program would have provided both individuals with similar opportunities for growth.

Significance

The desire to improve themselves not only impacted how they viewed their experience, but what they took from the program. If members had a desire to improve, they were more willing to go out and learn new things. One said, "Learning is inspiring me to learn more." They were more willing to go out of their comfort zone and gain new experiences. This played a major role in their confidence and overall service experience enjoyment. Another said, "The more I've learned the more confident I've become." If they were more willing to go out and capitalize on their new experiences, this shaped their view of themselves and the program.

Another significant aspect of this finding is that in many ways this kind of impact is out of the control of the program itself. The desire to for self-improvement is largely determined by the individual and not the program.

Proposed Program Response

- Recruitment: Program staff should identify applicants with characteristics that demonstrate an interest and willingness to for self-improvement through (a) including questions in the interview process and (b) stress the importance during career fairs and on written recruitment material.

- Self-Improvement plan: At the beginning of the term each member will set a self- improvement goal. Each month in their monthly reports they will set a goal and write out a plan on how they are going to improve themselves.

Finding #5 –Skillz that Pay the Billz

Description

Skill development was cited by our members as an integral part of their service experience. We expected job skill development, particularly personal energy efficiency, to be the most cited. What we found was that in addition to practical "hard" skills, members developed other "soft" skills, many of which were more durable and transferable to life after Green Iowa. These skills included effective communication, networking skills, decision-making, and leadership skills. Members learned a lot by working with others. "I was definitely able to more coherently grasp my own strengths and weaknesses as a leader working in a group." Particularly, being "forced" to work alongside homeowners, community members, and other GIAC team members—all whom have different communication and leadership styles—helped alumni develop more dynamic, flexible styles of their own.

Significance

The Green Iowa experience should be durable. Because many members do not always find a job in a field directly related to the work they do with Green Iowa, nurturing and developing skills that have fungibility across situation and occupation is critical. One participant said, "I always thought a skill had to be something you could do with your hands.... I didn't realize leadership was a skill I could get a job in." This ensures that no matter what path our members take after Green Iowa, alumni will contribute more positively and more effectively for their having served. From a programmatic standpoint this means we should place a bigger focus on skill development. Creating more opportunities for both "hard" and "soft" skill growth would be ideal.

Proposed Program Response

Weatherization Skills Test is an option to boost member skills. Such a test would be beneficial to both the producers and consumers of our service. Improving practical job skills serves to improve the quality of our product. Consumers of our service -- "at-risk" or "in-need" populations -- would reap the rewards of a more confident and able workforce. A weatherization skills test would also benefit our members, the producers of our service, particularly in pursuit of related career paths, such as energy auditing.

Additionally, increased job knowledge yields more confident members who are willing to take the lead on projects, who can be more effective evaluating problems, and who more willingly engage and network with other members of the community. Having a big effect requires having effective people.

Skill Transfer Training (STT) is another option to help members develop durable skills. An ongoing member-led STT program could benefit members in a number of ways. First, members would be able to teach to others skills at which they have some expertise, and through doing so utilize and grow their own communication and leadership skills. Secondly, attendees of these member-led seminars would have access to skills training they might not otherwise have on a daily basis. For non-member-led STTs, access to training conferences, workshops, or expert panels may also offer wonderful opportunities for member growth.

Out of Site, Out of Mind: All-Site gatherings might benefit skill development, build program coherence, and create enduring experiences for members. An experiment worth trying might be an overnight all-site retreat, or encouraging site-specific retreats at the very least. All-Site events bring together a diverse group of people with at least some degree of like-mindedness conducive to building a positive-growth environment.

Finding #6 – The Emotional Rollercoaster to Success

Description

Members and alumni both identified a heightened sense of emotional development as part of their service experience. Working in an organization that serves the less fortunate is bound to provide any person with a good dose of emotional highs and lows. Members are able to see people at their worst, in search of basic human needs. This creates a heightened sense of empathy and sensitivity to the world around them. One said, "I had never seen poverty that up close before. I just never knew people lived in those kind of conditions on daily basis before my AmeriCorps experience." Members and alumni indicated a greater sense of empathy and understanding for the world around them through the individuals they were able to help.

The program design provided members with an opportunity to emotionally develop in other areas, from pushing limits with new experiences to self-improvement through adversity. These are all things that members felt like the program, just by being what it is, provided them. The program was full of learning opportunities that open the eyes of members to the needs in ways they had not seen before. One said, "Once you know the condition of things, you feel a sense of obligation to take action. And if you don't take action, you have a sense of guilt."

Significance

The Green Iowa experience provides members with another life-skill that goes beyond environmental stewardship or nonprofit work. By creating opportunities for members to become more empathetic, more self-aware, more flexible and well adjusted, we are creating a better work force for any sector. Emotional development is a skill and area of growth that can be applied across the board and because of that, we have to be intentional in the way we incorporate it into our service work.

From a programmatic standpoint this means we should place a bigger focus on emotional development. We not only need to continue to create opportunities for emotional development but shine a spotlight on its importance.

Proposed Program Response

- Intentional Impact for Member Experience-Up to this point, program staff has not made any sort of conscious effort to raise awareness or emphasize emotional development. Instead of a pleasant side effect, evaluation of experiences and discussions will be geared around emotional development that can come from program service experiences
- Framing-Often times, stressful experiences, troubleshooting, difficult situations and unforeseen issues are seen as negative experiences. Through a process of framing and long-term growth these situations can be seen as silver lining moments for members continued emotional development.

Finding #7 – We the People

Description

An important theme we uncovered from alumni member responses was an amplified sense of civic obligation within the community. Members reported "feeling engaged and involved" within their communities while serving, but also within the communities in which they currently reside. The growing sense of obligation to become engaged was largely related to responses regarding an increase in confidence, values, and networking abilities. One said, "It gave me confidence to reach out to people in my new community by stepping outside my comfort zone." Alumni noted the value of connecting to the community through a variety of ways, including volunteering, speaking with other community members about an array of issues, and seeking out and attending community events.

Significance

Inspiring individuals to become involved in their communities is incredibly important for the sustainability and lifeline of the community itself. When community members are proactive and aware of issues facing our communities, they are better adept at confronting and solving those issues head on. One said, "I now go to town meetings and advocate for my community and neighbors. I feel like everyone is an important part of their community and even the small things we can do matter."

Becoming aware of ones' civic obligation can contribute to increased confidence and a sense of purpose and importance about one's place within the community. "I've realized that my presence in the community is important and can make a difference." Fostering members' sense of civic responsibility seems to have a significant positive impact on not only their own confidence, interpersonal skills, and self-worth, but also in the communities in which they are living and serving.

Proposed Program Response

Community Volunteering Hours: In addition to the monthly civic engagement training required by members, allowing a set number of hours each month for members to volunteer in various community sectors could also be helpful in fostering community engagement. Although our program focus is on energy conservation, allowing members to step outside this realm into community programs and events that consider other aspects of important civic issues, could help to broaden an individual's perspective on how they can become involved in their communities in a variety of ways that suit their own interests.

A COMMISSIONER'S PERSPECTIVE ON AMERICORPS SIP REPORTS

Nancy Franz, Ph.D.

As a commissioner for the Iowa Commission on Volunteer Service, I was delighted to be invited to read and hear program evaluation reports on the impact of the member experience for those providing service through AmeriCorps in my state. I served as program staff for the Youth Conservation Corps and Young Adult Conservation Corps so I know the value of the program and am thrilled to see that value being empirically documented.

The AmeriCorps program evaluations I read and listened to were well done. I was impressed with the quality of the qualitative data on the benefits of the member experience rather than the random anecdotal stories that are often communicated. This systematic and deep collection of qualitative data easily supplements and enhances the quantitative data collected for program performance measures. This alternative way to explore and report program impact clearly highlighted not only the impact of the AmeriCorps member experience but also the benefits and potential changes for the host experience and the program administrative experience all linked to the overall expected goals and outcomes for the program.

In listening to the program reports it was heartening to hear the benefits articulated of the participatory approach used throughout the evaluation. Program staff had fun learning about the science and art of program evaluation. More importantly they learned the value of critical reflection for better understanding, improving, and communicating about their programs. The staff are already thinking about and planning for ways to use their newly acquired evaluative thinking, practices, and tools to work in additional ways to improve their programs. This participatory approach to program evaluation has helped them realize the value of a more holistic approach to their work rather than just carrying out the day-to-day activities of program implementation. Instead of just measuring program processes, they are also measuring human performance and program products.

For over three decades I've conducted and assisted with a variety of public program evaluations. Through the SIP reports, I continue to see immense value of evaluation self-studies especially for AmeriCorps programs that implement programs across a wide variety of contexts. Self-studies are not only effective but help keep costs low for evaluation, build program staff evaluation capacity, and reveal methodologies and findings that are context specific. Valuable intended and unintended program outcomes are often deeply documented in these types of studies. Evaluation self-studies provide a great opportunity to build personal and program awareness and capacity of what works and does not work about a program for continuous program improvement and professional development for AmeriCorps members, staff, and host organizations.

As I read and heard these program evaluation reports from these AmeriCorps programs in Iowa several themes caught my eye and ear:

- The affirmation of past findings of AmeriCorps program evaluation and research
- Deeper understanding of AmeriCorps and the program brand and identity
- The building of member confidence by pushing and stretching the member, client, and partners
- The presence of important unintended impacts/findings

- An increase in the depth and scope of the program through a multiplier effect of member efforts
- The centrality of learning throughout the member experience and the benefit to host organizations
- Building evaluation capacity and joy through the self-study process and related coaching

After hearing these themes I suggested a variety of next steps for these programs to consider. I called it the "So what, what?." Program staff need to determine how their evaluation findings can support the overall goals and measures of their host organization. They also need to think about how their findings change how they talk about their programs and how they can be more intentional about their programming through critical reflection. I call this the "evaluate, share, change, evaluate" cycle. I suggested they find more visual ways to share their findings that are audience specific. For example what I most often heard was a formula for success that could be illustrated as "member skills + host mentoring = program success." I also encouraged them to use data visualization techniques and more fully integrate qualitative and quantitative findings in describing their programs. They can also improve the believability of and confidence in their findings by tying it to existing research. Finally, I suggested they continue learning from each other as program staff and more fully involve AmeriCorps alumni as member coaches to enhance their findings and impact.

For those reading this important monograph, I invite you to take action to continue to improve AmeriCorps and similar programs:

- Advocate for the value of qualitative self-studies and mixed methods (qualitative and quantitative) studies to help determine program impact. Randomized control trials or return on investment studies are often not viable for small, rural, and minimally funded AmeriCorps programs
- Ensure that at least 10% of program budgets are dedicated for program evaluation. Some evaluation designs such as randomized control trials can consume 50% or more of a program budget.

- Support program evaluation capacity building of AmeriCorps staff and host organizations to promote evaluative thinking and action that improves personal and program performance as well as deeper and wider program impact.

- Stress the need for a wide variety of program success measures across environmental, social, and economic changes. Evaluation focus is often times overly focused just on economic measures.

- Help stakeholders remember that AmeriCorps is about volunteer service and the benefits of that service to individuals, communities, and our nation. Oftentimes the program is valued only for the program outcomes and the volunteer benefits are unheard.

- Promote program evaluation at all stages of program needs assessment, design, and implementation rather than waiting to consider evaluation after a program is well underway.

- Work closely with program evaluation expert practitioners to help plan, implement, and share appropriate program evaluation designs, lessons learned, and insights. Don't go it alone!

I greatly appreciate the hard work of the program staff and the evaluation experts who produced this amazing monograph about the impact of the AmeriCorps member experience. I hope you find it a valuable opportunity for critical reflection and related action to improve your programs.